# ᴛʜᴇQuotable
# DRUNKARD

# THE Quotable DRUNKARD

WORDS OF WIT, WISDOM, and PHILOSOPHY from the BOTTOM of the GLASS

STEVEN KATES

**A**adamsmedia
Avon, Massachusetts

Published by
Adams Media, a division of F+W Media, Inc.
57 Littlefield Street, Avon, MA 02322. U.S.A.
*www.adamsmedia.com*

ISBN 10: 1-4405-1264-7
ISBN 13: 978-1-4405-1264-3
eISBN 10: 1-4405-2180-8
eISBN 13: 978-1-4405-2180-5

Printed in the United States of America.

10  9  8  7  6  5  4  3  2  1

**Library of Congress Cataloging-in-Publication Data**
is available from the publisher.

This publication is designed to provide accurate and authoritative information with regard to the subject matter covered. It is sold with the understanding that the publisher is not engaged in rendering legal, accounting, or other
professional advice. If legal advice or other expert assistance is required, the
services of a competent professional person should be sought.
—From a *Declaration of Principles* jointly adopted by a Committee of the
American Bar Association and a Committee of Publishers and Associations

Many of the designations used by manufacturers and sellers to distinguish
their product are claimed as trademarks. Where those designations appear in
this book and Adams Media was aware of a trademark claim, the designations
have been printed with initial capital letters.

All interior illustrations © Jupiterimages Corporation

*This book is available at quantity discounts for bulk purchases.*
*For information, please call 1-800-289-0963.*

# DEDICATION

To Your Health

# CONTENTS

## Part I
### I Drink, Therefore I Am • 1

## Part II
### Celebration, Intoxication, Regurgitation • 87

## Part III
### The Wisdom of Wine (and Beer and Liquor) • 185

# PART I

# I DRINK, THEREFORE I AM

CHAPTER 1

# IN THE BEGINNING, THERE WAS ALCOHOL— AND IT WAS GOOD

To paraphrase a rhyme from elementary school: "God makes the rivers, God makes the lakes, Man makes booze, and we all make mistakes."

Religious texts such as the Hebrew Bible and Christian New Testament have plenty to say about alcohol, but before you assume that their philosophy can be expressed in one word—"don't"—take heed, my brothers and sisters, to the following passages. Therein thou shalt see that the drinking of wine and strong drink is not itself a sin in the eyes of the Lord: rather, it is drunkenness, dissipation, and excess on which the Creator frowns, for such behavior abuses the gifts of the earth and the temple of the body and leads to sinful behavior such as lewdness, dancing, and beer sliding.

Let us begin with "case against" quotations and end on the happy note of "case for."

## The Case Against

"Deacons, likewise, are to be men worthy of respect, sincere, not indulging in much wine, and not pursuing dishonest gain."

—1 Timothy 3:8

"Get up, go away!
    For this is not your resting place,
    Because it is defiled,
    It is ruined, beyond all remedy.
    If a liar and deceiver comes and says,
    'I will prophesy for you plenty of wine and beer,'
    He would be just the prophet for this people!"

—Micah 2:10–11

**POTABLE QUOTABLE**

In the book of Genesis, Lot's two daughters mistakenly believe that the destruction of Sodom and Gomorrah means the annihilation of all humankind, so they take it upon themselves to repopulate the earth: they get their father drunk and have sex with him. Twice. Lot's older daughter tells her sister, "Come, let us make our father drink wine, and we will lie with him, that we may preserve seed of our father." Years of family therapy ensue.

"Woe to those who rise early in the morning
    To run after their drinks,
    Who stay up late at night
    Till they are inflamed with wine.
    They have harps and lyres at their banquets,
    Tambourines and flutes and wine,
    But they have no regard for the deeds of the LORD,
    No respect for the work of his hands."

—Isaiah 5:10–12

"Harlotry, wine and new wine take away the understanding."

—Hosea 4:11

## THE DRINKS CABINET

Every now and then you see commercials for beer or wine companies whose noble traditions go back all the way to 1984 or even 1884. If you want a drink that's stood the test of time, ask for mead: a wine made from honey, with origins in China somewhere around, oh, 7000 B.C.E. Since then, mead has fueled drinking parties in India, Europe, and Africa, finding particular favor among Vikings and men who sing battle anthems. Today, mead comes carbonated, sparkling, sweet, or semisweet, and may be enhanced with fruit, spices, or even chili peppers or maple syrup. Alcohol content varies, but the constant is honey, honey.

"Wine is a mocker, strong drink a brawler / and whoever is intoxicated by it is not wise."

—PROVERBS 20:1

"Choose Christ! And there'll never be a hangover but joy and peace."

—REV. BILLY GRAHAM

"God doesn't want us to cloud or confuse our minds in any way, whether with drugs, alcohol, or anything else."

—REV. BILLY GRAHAM

"He who loves pleasure will become poor; whoever loves wine and oil will never be rich."

—PROVERBS 21:17

## POTABLE QUOTABLE

The Holy Bible has several instances of people assuming drunkenness on the part of those who relate some transcendent religious experience. In the second chapter of Acts of the Apostles, the Holy Spirit descends on Jesus' followers and they all begin preaching in different languages. Some members of the crowd think the apostles "have had too much wine," but Peter reproves them, saying, "These men are not drunk, as you suppose. It is only nine in the morning!" Well, you can't argue with logic like that.

"Do not be with heavy drinkers of wine,
   Or with gluttonous eaters of meat;
   For the heavy drinker and the glutton will come to poverty,
   And drowsiness will clothe one with rags."

—PROVERBS 23:20–21

"Who has woe? Who has sorrow?
   Who has contentions? Who has complaining?
   Who has wounds without cause?
   Who has redness of eyes?
   Those who linger long over wine,
   Those who go to taste mixed wine."

—PROVERBS 23:29–30

## "I prefer to think that God is not dead, just drunk."

—JOHN MARCELLUS HUSTON

## POTABLE QUOTABLE

In the book of Daniel, King Belshazzar is not content to use his wedding crystal: he orders that wine be served in "the gold and silver goblets that Nebuchadnezzar his father had taken from the temple in Jerusalem," which prompts the party of nobles and concubines to praise "the gods of gold and silver, of bronze, iron, wood and stone." That night, an omen proclaimed that the dissolute king had been tried and found wanting. Shortly thereafter, he was killed. Let that be a lesson that it matters not only what you serve, but what you serve it in.

"If in thirst you drink water from a cup, you see God in it. Those who are not in love with God will see only their own faces in it."

—RUMI MEVIANA

# "There is a devil in every berry of the grape."

—THE KORAN

"And these also reel with wine and stagger from strong drink:

The priest and the prophet reel with strong drink,

They are confused by wine, they stagger from strong drink;

They reel while having visions,

They totter when rendering judgment.

For all the tables are full of filthy vomit, without a single clean place.

All the tables are covered with vomit, and there is not a spot without filth."

—ISAIAH 28:7–8

"Do not look on the wine when it is red,

When it sparkles in the cup,

When it goes down smoothly;

At the last it bites like a serpent

And stings like a viper.

Your eyes will see strange things

And your mind will utter perverse things."

—PROVERBS 23:29–35

After the flood, Noah plants a vineyard and gets so drunk on its wine that he passes out naked in his tent. When Noah learns that his son Ham has seen his nakedness, he curses Ham's son Canaan: "Cursed be Canaan! The lowest of slaves will he be to his brothers!" Talk about a mean drunk!

"Woe to those who are heroes at drinking wine and champions at mixing drinks, who acquit the guilty for a bribe, but deny justice to the innocent."

—ISAIAH 5:22–23

"No longer do they drink wine with a song; the beer is bitter to its drinkers."

—ISAIAH 24:9

"They are dogs with mighty appetites; they never have enough. They are shepherds who lack understanding; they all turn to their own way, each seeks his own gain. 'Come,' each one cries, 'let me get wine! Let us drink our fill of beer! And tomorrow will be like today, or even far better.'"

—ISAIAH 56:11–12

"Be stunned and amazed, blind yourselves and be sightless; be drunk, but not from wine, stagger, but not from beer."

—ISAIAH 29:9

"Their wine is the venom of serpents, the deadly poison of cobras."

—DEUTERONOMY 32:33

"Speak to the Israelites and say to them: 'If a man or woman wants to make a special vow, a vow of separation to the LORD as a Nazarite, he must abstain from wine and other fermented drink and must not drink vinegar made from wine or from other fermented drink. He must not drink grape juice or eat grapes or raisins. As long as he is a Nazarite, he must not eat anything that comes from the grapevine, not even the seeds or skins."

—NUMBERS 6:2–4

"In the hand of the LORD is a cup full of foaming wine mixed with spices; he pours it out, and all the wicked of the earth drink it down to its very dregs."

—PSALM 75:8

"It is better not to eat meat or drink wine or to do anything else that will cause your brother to fall."

—ROMANS 14:21

"They cast lots for my people and traded boys for prostitutes; they sold girls for wine that they might drink."

—JOEL 3:3

"Hannah was praying in her heart, and her lips were moving but her voice was not heard. Eli thought she was drunk and said to her, 'How long will you keep on getting drunk? Get rid of your wine.'

'Not so, my lord,' Hannah replied, 'I am a woman who is deeply troubled. I have not been drinking wine or beer; I was pouring out my soul to the LORD.'"

—1 Samuel 1:13–15

**WATERING SPOTS**

The oldest—and still-operating—U.S. vineyard dedicated exclusively to producing sacramental wine is O-Neh-Da Vineyards (est. 1872), located in the Finger Lakes region of New York State. The vineyard's founder was Roman Catholic Bishop Bernard McQuaid, who, according to the vineyard's website, "chose the name O·Neh·Da to respect the native [American] given name for Hemlock Lake." O-Neh-Da Vineyards sells sacramental wines to churches only, but should you want a taste of their grape, they have the division Eagle Crest Vineyards, which is succulently secular.

"Then the Lord awoke as from sleep, as a man wakes from the stupor of wine. He beat back his enemies; he put them to everlasting shame."

—Psalm 78:65–66

"Do not get drunk on wine, which leads to debauchery. Instead, be filled with the Spirit."

—Ephesians 5:18

"Wake up, you drunkards, and weep! Wail, all you drinkers of wine; wail because of the new wine, for it has been snatched from your lips."

—JOEL 1:5

"It is not for kings, O Lemuel— not for kings to drink wine, not for rulers to crave beer,

Lest they drink and forget what the law decrees, and deprive all the oppressed of their rights.

Give beer to those who are perishing, wine to those who are in anguish;

Let them drink and forget their poverty and remember their misery no more."

—PROVERBS 31:4–7

**POTABLE QUOTABLES**

According to the book of Matthew, Jesus at his crucifixion was offered something to drink: "There they offered Jesus wine to drink, mixed with gall; but after tasting it, he refused to drink it." The word *gall* in Greek means "poison," so either someone was trying to slip Jesus a Mickey or was trying to put him out of his misery. Having tasted the bitterness of the poison, Jesus likely refused the drink because he did not want his death to be a suicide.

Later, Jesus refuses to drink wine vinegar: he may have been adhering to scripture, which forbade anyone from drinking wine before entering God's temple.

"Woe to him who gives drink to his neighbors, pouring it from the wineskin till they are drunk, so that he can gaze on their naked bodies."

—HABAKKUK 2:15

"But now I am writing you that you must not associate with anyone who calls himself a brother but is sexually immoral or greedy, an idolater or a slanderer, a drunkard or a swindler. With such a man do not even eat."

—1 CORINTHIANS 5:11

## THE DRINKS CABINET

Not a few potent potables were invented by clergy, particularly monks. Either to honor that tradition or to lend their product an aura of saintliness, some alcoholic beverages are named after holy people. Why not consider one of these, when getting a gift for your spiritual counselor?

- **Frangelico.** Hazelnut liqueur named after Italian painter Fra Angelico, bottle shaped like a monk
- **Blue Nun.** Out-of-fashion, moderately priced German wine
- **Saint Brendan's Irish Cream Liqueur.** Made in Ireland, naturally
- **St.-Germain.** French liqueur made from elderflowers
- **Bénédictine.** Herbal liqueur made in France

"You and your sons are not to drink wine or other fermented drink whenever you go into the Tent of Meeting, or you will die. This is a lasting ordinance for the generations to come."

—LEVITICUS 10:9

## THE CASE FOR! (MAKE THAT TWO CASES OR MORE)

"If God had intended us to drink beer, He would have given us stomachs."

—DAVID DAYE

"Man's way to God is with beer in hand."

—NIGERIAN PROVERB

"You have filled my heart with greater joy than when their grain and new wine abound."

—PSALM 4:7

"May God give you of

heaven's dew and of

earth's richness—an

abundance of grain

and new wine."

—GENESIS 27:28

"Alcohol may be man's worst enemy, but the Bible says love your enemy."

—FRANK SINATRA

*Mrs. Fenty*: You should read the Bible, Mr. Rumson.

*Ben Rumson*: I have read the Bible, Mrs. Fenty.

*Mrs. Fenty*: Didn't that discourage you about drinking?

*Ben Rumson*: No, but it sure killed my appetite for readin'!

—*PAINT YOUR WAGON*

"Your navel is a rounded goblet that never lacks blended wine."

—Song of Solomon 7:2

"[The LORD God] makes grass grow for the cattle,
And plants for man to cultivate
Bringing forth food from the earth:
Wine that gladdens the heart of man,
Oil to make his face shine,
And bread that sustains his heart."

—Psalm 104:14–16

"Go, eat your food with gladness, and drink your wine with a joyful heart, for it is now that God favors what you do."

—Ecclesiastes 9:7

"Let him kiss me with the kisses of his mouth—for your love is more delightful than wine."

—Song of Solomon 1:2

"Grain will make the young men thrive, / and new wine the young women."

—ZECHARIAH 9:17

Bible, the Lord God promises "new wine" for the people: a new message of love, hope, and promise.

"My drinking is directly connected to my smoking. Now, when I say 'directly,' I mean there's a thing—a physical thing—that is directly connected from my liquor buds to the smoke pouch in my lungs. . . . Do you understand, Reverman? The booze bone's connected to the smoke bone. And the smoke bone's connected to the head bone. And that's the word of the Lord!"

—EDGAR STOPWORTH, *COLD TURKEY*

## POTABLE QUOTABLES

The evangelist John cites Jesus' first miracle at a wedding in a village in southern Lebanon called Cana: "When the wine was gone, Jesus' mother said to him, 'They have no more wine.'" No problemo: water becomes wine. Among the many ways to interpret Jesus' miracle is to consider that ordinary people can perform this "miracle": vintners, after all, turn water into wine. Perhaps what Jesus is saying is that we all have the potential to transform and to be transformed. In the Hebrew

"A man hath no better thing under the sun, than to eat, and to drink, and to be merry."

—ECCLESIASTES 8:15

*Reverend Hood*: And now for my next trick, the *pièce de resistance*, I present to you an empty glass. I will now fill this glass with milk . . .

*Chris*: Would it work better with whiskey, Vicar?

*Reverend Hood*: Nothing works better with whiskey.

*Tom*: I do!

*Reverend Hood*: You've never worked a day in your life, Tom.

—*STRAW DOGS*

"On this mountain the LORD Almighty will prepare a feast of rich food for all peoples, a banquet of aged wine—the best of meats and the finest of wines."

—ISAIAH 25:6

# "Eat, O friends, and drink; drink your fill, O lovers."

—SONG OF SOLOMON 5:1

**POTABLE QUOTABLE**

Chances are, you had to read John Steinbeck's novel *The Grapes of Wrath* in high school, so you probably know that the title comes from a line in the Civil War-era song "The Battle Hymn of the Republic" by Julia Ward Howe. What you may not know is that Howe was inspired by a passage in the New Testament's book of Revelation, describing an apocalyptic vision: "And the angel thrust in his sickle into the earth, and gathered the vine of the earth, and cast it into the great winepress of the wrath of God. And the winepress was trodden without the city, and blood came out of the winepress, even unto the horse bridles, by the space of a thousand and six hundred furlongs." (Revelations 14:19–20)

"Come, all you who are thirsty, come to the waters; and you who have no money, come, buy and eat! Come, buy wine and milk without money and without cost."

—ISAIAH 55:1

# "Woman first tempted man to eat; he took to drinking of his own accord."

—JOHN R. KEMBLE

## THE DRINKS CABINET

Count your blessings, we are told. Good advice, so let's start with thanking heaven that some European monks had time to invent alcoholic drinks we enjoy today. Will imbibing these drinks give you a religious experience? There's only one way to find out for sure, my brothers and sisters.

- **Champagne.** Allegedly discovered by Benedictine monk Dom Perignon (1638–1715) who is said to have exclaimed, "Come quickly, I am drinking the stars!" Both attributions are false: Benedictine monks were making sparkling wine about 100 years before Perignon was born, and the "drinking stars" remark is from a nineteenth-century ad.
- **Chartreuse.** An herbal liqueur invented by the Carthusian monks of the Grande Chartreuse Monastery of France. Manufactured in both a yellow and green variety, chartreuse appears in *The Great Gatsby* and in Quentin Tarantino's movie *Death Proof.* Versatile!
- **Buckfast Tonic Wine.** A caffeinated, sweet, inexpensive fortified wine courtesy of Benedictine monks of Buckfast Abbey in Devon, England, this potent potable (15 percent alcohol) is notorious for greasing the wheels of many a soccer brawl and Scottish "exchange of views."

"But see, there is joy and revelry, slaughtering of cattle and killing of sheep, eating of meat and drinking of wine! 'Let us eat and drink,' you say, 'for tomorrow we die!'"

—ISAIAH 22:13

CHAPTER 2

# BEER, GLORIOUS BEER!

According to respected historians and barflies, the only drink more ancient than beer is water (and with some "light" brands of beer, it may be hard to tell the difference). Television commercials have educated us well on the basics of what makes beer: a fermented blend of barley, wheat, and the magical ingredient hops, which is where we get the term "barhopping."

At least that's what this guy on the stool next to me told me one time.

Beer comes in bottles, barrels, cans, casks, balls, kegs, half-kegs, and funnels held at roughly a ninety-degree angle. Beer is the drink that makes baseball interesting, plain people beautiful, and dull ones philosophers. Beer is the traditional drink before a chaser, and it greases the engine of friendship the world over. Here's to suds, stouts, pale ales, porters, lagers, and beer lovers everywhere!

"He was a wise man who invented beer."

—PLATO

"It's beer o'clock and I'm buying."

—TEDDY, *MEMENTO*

"Guys! I apologize in advance for any incivility or insensitivity on my part, but it is beer o'clock."

—JOHN CRICHTON, *FARSCAPE*

"Right, find out who that dead woman was, find out who killed her. Do it now. [*checks his watch*] Hold on, hold on. Do it tomorrow morning first thing. Beer o'clock, gentlemen."

—GENE HUNT, *LIFE ON MARS*

"Wow, I just drank a beer! Who wants to do me?"

—CARTOON LINDSAY LOHAN, "I DREAM OF JESUS," *FAMILY GUY*

"God has a brown voice, as soft and full as beer."

—ANNE SEXTON

"If you ever reach total enlightenment while drinking beer, I bet it makes beer shoot out your nose."

—JACK HANDEY

"Where does one not find that bland degeneration which beer produces in the spirit!"

—FRIEDRICH NIETZSCHE

"Many battles have been fought and won by soldiers nourished on beer."

—FREDERICK THE GREAT

"Oh no! What have I done? I smashed open my little boy's piggy bank, and for what? A few measly cents, not even enough to buy one beer. Wait a minute, lemme count and make sure . . . not even close."

—HOMER SIMPSON,
THE SIMPSONS

"Draft beer, not people."

—ANONYMOUS

"Man seeks to escape himself in myth, and does so by any means at his disposal. Drugs, alcohol, or lies. Unable to withdraw into himself, he disguises himself. Lies and inaccuracy give him a few moments of comfort."

—JEAN COCTEAU

"Bring in the bottled lightning, a clean tumbler, and a corkscrew."

—CHARLES DICKENS

"Ale, man, ale's the stuff to drink for fellows whom it hurts to think."

—A. E. HOUSMAN

"Better belly burst than good liquor be lost."

—JONATHAN SWIFT

"Some men are like musical glasses; to produce their finest tones you must keep them wet."

—SAMUEL TAYLOR COLERIDGE

"Most Americans are born drunk, and really require a little wine or beer to sober them. They have a sort of permanent intoxication from within, a sort of invisible champagne. Americans do not need to drink to inspire them to do anything, though they do sometimes, I think, need a little for the deeper and more delicate purpose of teaching them how to do nothing."

—G. K. CHESTERTON

"There is this to be said in favor of drinking, that it takes the drunkard first out of society, then out of the world."

—RALPH WALDO EMERSON

"Drink not the third glass, which thou canst not tame, when once it is within thee."

—GEORGE HERBERT

"I always drank, from when it was legal for me to drink. And there was never a time for me when the goal wasn't to get as hammered as I could possibly afford to. I never understood social drinking: that's always seemed to me like kissing your sister."

—STEPHEN KING

"What marriage is to morality, a properly conducted licensed liquor traffic is to sobriety."

—MARK TWAIN

"When you go out with a drunk, you'll notice how a drunk fills your glass so he can empty his own. As long as you're drinking, drinking is okay. Two's company. Drinking is fun. If there's a bottle, even if your glass isn't empty, he'll pour a little in your glass before he fills his own."

—CHUCK PALAHNIUK

"Sobriety diminishes, discriminates, and says no; drunkenness expands, unites, and says yes. Not through mere perversity do men run after it."

—WILLIAM JAMES

"Bacchus ever fair and young,
  Drinking joys did first ordain.
Bacchus's blessings are a treasure,
Drinking is the soldier's pleasure,
Rich the treasure,
Sweet the pleasure—
Sweet is pleasure after pain."

—JOHN DRYDEN

"Under a bad cloak there is often a good drinker."

—MIGUEL DE CERVANTES

"Drink moderately, for drunkenness neither keeps a secret, nor observes a promise."

—MIGUEL DE CERVANTES

"Sobriety, severity, and self-respect are the foundations of all true sociality."

—HENRY DAVID THOREAU

"Our national drug is alcohol. We tend to regard the use of any other drug with special horror."

—WILLIAM S. BURROUGHS

"No animal ever invented anything as bad as drunkenness—or as good as drink."

—G. K. CHESTERTON

# "Perfect reason flees all extremity and leads one to be wise with sobriety."

—MOLIÈRE

"The sway of alcohol over mankind is unquestionably due to its power to stimulate the mystical faculties of human nature, usually crushed to earth by the cold facts and dry criticisms of the sober hour."

—WILLIAM JAMES

"Two great European narcotics: alcohol and Christianity."

—FRIEDRICH NIETZSCHE

"It was my Uncle George who discovered that alcohol was a food well in advance of modern medical thought."

—P. G. WODEHOUSE

"Anyway, no drug, not even alcohol, causes the fundamental ills of society. If we're looking for the source of our troubles, we shouldn't test people for drugs, we should test them for stupidity, ignorance, greed, and love of power."

—P. J. O'ROURKE

"It is not heroin or cocaine that makes one an addict, it is the need to escape from a harsh reality. There are more television addicts, more baseball and football addicts, more movie addicts, and certainly more alcohol addicts in this country than there are narcotics addicts."

—SHIRLEY CHISHOLM

"Man being reasonable must get drunk;
　The best of life is but intoxication;
　Glory, the grape, love, gold, in these are sunk
　The hopes of all men and of every nation."

—LORD BYRON

"Be wary of strong drink. It can make you shoot at tax collectors . . . and miss."

—ROBERT HEINLEIN

"Sometimes when I reflect back on all the beer I drink I feel ashamed. Then I look into the glass and think about the workers in the brewery and all of their hopes and dreams. If I didn't drink this beer, they might be out of work and their dreams would be shattered. Then I say to myself, it is better that I drink this beer and let their dreams come true than be selfish and worry about my liver."

—JACK HANDEY

"Beer! Now *there's* a temporary solution!"

—HOMER SIMPSON,
*THE SIMPSONS*

"Beer is not a good cocktail party drink, especially in a home where you don't know where the bathroom is."

—BILLY CARTER

"There is nothing for a case of nerves like a case of beer."

—JOAN GOLDSTEIN

"I've always believed that paradise will have my favorite beer on tap."

—RUDYARD WHEATLEY

"Do not cease to drink beer, to eat, to intoxicate thyself, to make love, and celebrate the good days."

—EGYPTIAN PROVERB

"Praise not the day until evening has come; a woman until she is burnt; a sword until it is tried; a maiden until she is married; ice until it has been crossed; beer until it has been drunk."

—NORSE PROVERB

"A statesman is an easy man: he tells his lies by rote. A journalist invents his lies, and rams them down your throat. So stay at home and drink your beer and let the neighbors vote."

—W. B. YEATS

# "When I die I want to decompose in a barrel of porter and have it served in all the pubs in Ireland."

—J. P. DONLEAVY

"They who drink beer will think beer."

—WASHINGTON IRVING

"I have a total irreverence for anything connected with society, except that which makes the roads safer, the beer stronger, the old men and women warmer in the winter, and happier in the summer."

—BRENDAN BEHAN

"The mouth of a perfectly happy man is filled with beer."

—EGYPTIAN PROVERB

"Not all chemicals are bad. Without chemicals such as hydrogen and oxygen, for example, there would be no way to make water, a vital ingredient in beer."

—DAVE BARRY

"I like beer. On occasion, I will even drink beer to celebrate a major event such as the fall of Communism or the fact that the refrigerator is still working."

—DAVE BARRY

"Life, alas, is very drear. Up with the glass, down with the beer!"

—LOUIS UNTERMEYER

"Beer makes you feel the way you ought to feel without beer."

—HENRY LAWSON

"The best beer in the world is the open bottle in your hand!"

—DANNY JANSEN

"Twenty-four hours in a day, twenty-four beers in a case. Coincidence?"

—STEPHEN WRIGHT

"Ah, good ol' trustworthy beer. My love for you will never die."

—HOMER SIMPSON, THE SIMPSONS

"Not one man in a

beer commercial has

a beer belly."

—RITA RUDNER

"I would rather commit adultery than drink a glass of beer."

—LADY ASTOR

"Here's to a long life and a merry one! A quick death and an easy one! A pretty girl and an honest one! A cold beer—and another one!"

—IRISH TOAST

"Men are nicotine-soaked, beer-besmirched, whiskey-greased, red-eyed devils."

—CARRIE NATION

"Give me a woman who loves beer and I will conquer the world."

—KAISER WILHELM

"Bart, a woman is like beer. They look good, they smell good, and you'd step over your own mother just to get one!"

—HOMER SIMPSON,
THE SIMPSONS

"Beauty is in the eye of the beer holder."

—ANONYMOUS

## THE DRINKS CABINET

Diluting, or "cutting," beer with a second beverage is done either to lower the drink's alcohol content, play with its flavor, or invent a new libation. Here are some of the more popular beer mixes and their oddball names:

- **Panaché (France) [pah-nah-SHAY]:** Beer and lemon-flavored soda/soda water
- **Monaco (France):** Panaché and grenadine
- **Shandy (UK):** Beer and lemonade. In the UK, the lemonade is carbonated.
- **Shandygaff (UK):** Beer and ginger ale, or ginger beer
- **Lager Top (UK):** 80 percent beer, 20 percent carbonated lemonade
- **Potsdamer (Germany):** Pilsner beer and flavored soda with a shot of raspberry syrup
- **Demi-Peche (France) [dem-ee-PESH]:** Beer with a shot of peach-flavored syrup
- **Radler (Germany):** Beer and soda pop, or beer and lemonade.
- **Diesel (UK):** Beer and cider with a splash of crème de cassis
- **Snakebite (UK, US):** Beer and cider
- **Gespritzer (Germany) [guh-SHPRITS-uh]:** Beer and cola

- **Black Shandy (UK, US):** Guinness and lemonade
- **Cincinnati (US):** Beer and lemon-lime soda (e.g., Sprite)

"Without question, the greatest invention in the history of mankind is beer. Oh, I grant you that the wheel was also a fine invention, but the wheel does not go nearly as well with pizza."

—DAVE BARRY

"The white sheet bleaching on the hedge,
    With heigh! The sweet birds, O, how they sing!
    Doth set my pugging tooth on edge;
    For a quart of ale is a dish for a king."

—AUTOLYCUS, *A WINTER'S TALE*, WILLIAM SHAKESPEARE

"People who drink light 'beer' don't like the taste of beer; they just like to pee a lot."

—CAPITAL BREWERY, WI

"Beer needs baseball, and baseball needs beer—it has always been thus."

—PETER RICHMOND

"Be brave, then; for your captain is brave, and vows reformation. . . . I will make it felony to drink small beer."

—CADE, *KING HENRY VI*, WILLIAM SHAKESPEARE

"Would I were in an alehouse in London! I would give all my fame for a pot of ale and safety."

—BOY, *KING HENRY V*, WILLIAM SHAKESPEARE

"You can't be a real country unless you have a beer and an airline—it helps if you have some kind of a football team, or some nuclear weapons, but at the very least you need a beer."

—FRANK ZAPPA

## THE DRINKS CABINET

If you feel like punching up your beer a bit, just add more alcohol and voilà! A new drink. Bartending with beer is easier than you think.

- **Boilermaker (US):** Beer with a shot of vodka or tequila
- **Sake Bomb (US) [SOCK-ee bomb]:** A shot of Japanese rice wine poured or dropped into a pint of beer
- **Turbo Shandy (US, UK):** Beer and alcoholic lemonade (e.g., Mike's Hard Lemonade)
- **Black and Tan (UK, US):** Pale ale and stout
- **Black Velvet (UK, US):** Guinness stout and champagne
- **Porchcrawler (US):** Beer, vodka, and lemonade concentrate
- **Uboot (Germany) [YOU-boot]:** Beer and vodka. In Russia, this is a "Yorsh."

"A little bit of beer is divine medicine."

—PARACELSUS, GREEK
PHYSICIAN

"I'm sick, Tom. I need a cure: vitamin B cocktail, followed by an amp of glucose and a drop of adrenaline. Not as good as beer, but it's all I got."

—FRANK PIERCE, *BRINGING OUT THE DEAD*

*Malone*: How'd you like a nice tall glass of ice cold beer?

*Potts*: Beer! Strictly a middle class beverage. The last time I was back in Brooklyn, there was just such a night as this. We was havin' cocktails. My old lady brought 'em in, I took one taste, and boy what a kick. You know what she did?

*Malone*: What?

*Potts*: She took 'em out and put in another slug of gin. What a sweet old lady.

—*GUADALCANAL DIARY*

"Beer, if drunk with moderation, softens the temper, cheers the spirit, and promotes health."

—THOMAS JEFFERSON

"I don't believe this. You're taking advice from Oswald? Oswald who once swallowed a sponge to soak up all the beer, so he won't get drunk?"

—KATE O'BRIEN, *THE DREW CAREY SHOW*

"I learned early on that passion, stupidity and eighty ounces of cheap beer will win the heart of any woman. And if it doesn't, you'll be too *hammered* to remember."

—CHRISTOPHER TITUS, *TITUS*

*Jan Wolfhouse*: So yeah, I heard you got fired from the brewery?

*Landfill*: Goddamn brewery! You know that brewery makes 10,000 bottles of beer a day. I drink 45 of them, and *I'm* the asshole!

—*BEERFEST*

*Lois*: Why do you care so much about touring a stupid brewery?

*Peter*: Lois, everyone has their sanctuary. The Catholics have churches, fat people have Wisconsin, and I have the Pawtucket Brewery. Now, now help me drink these beers.

—*FAMILY GUY*

*Junior Shop Assistant*: Why do girls like you always have a boyfriend?

*Susan Walker*: Because I have acute nymphomania and my own brewery.

—*COUPLING*

## THE DRINKS CABINET

Hobnob in microbrew pubs long enough (say, ten minutes) and you are bound to hear discussion of "real ale," which, if you've never heard the term, may make you wonder if ginger ale qualifies as "fake ale."

Nope. "Real ale" refers to the methods by which beer is made, fermented, stored, and dispensed. If your ale does not use chemicals, preservatives, or additives and instead relies on what connoisseurs call "traditional ingredients"; if it is unfiltered and unpasteurized; if the yeast is still active and conditioning the beer; and if it is served without the use of carbon dioxide, then you're drinking the real stuff.

"But Uncle Red, you cannot make a fine quality lager using Kool-Aid technology!"

—HAROLD, *THE RED GREEN SHOW*

*Red Green*: You know, the ancient Romans brewed beer, Harold. In fact, every great Western civilization brewed beer. Did you know that?

*Harold*: Yes, I did. And did you know that, at some point, every great civilization collapsed? Connection, perhaps?

*Red Green*: Harold, if it's good enough for Julius Caesar, it's good enough for Possum Lodge.

*Harold*: *Veni, vidi, vomiti.* I came, I saw, I ralphed.

—THE RED GREEN SHOW

**POTABLE QUOTABLES**

"Beer is evidence that God loves us and wants us to be happy," attributed to Ben Franklin, is one of the most quoted celebrity endorsements of beer. The quote looks good on a T-shirt, but that's not what ol' Ben said.

In 1779, Franklin wrote a letter to André Morelet, a French economist and author, in which he noted: "Behold the rain which descends from heaven upon our vineyards, there it enters the roots of the vines, to be changed into wine, a constant proof that God loves us, and loves to see us happy."

*Peter Griffin* [*trying to potty-train Stewie*] You know, I oughtta just give you some beer. Goes straight through you.

Stewie: [sarcastic] Wonderful. And while we're at it, we can light up a doobie and watch porn.

*Peter*: Eh . . . yeah?

—FAMILY GUY

"OK, guys. I don't have any beer. I hate alcohol, and I won't have it in my house. So, we're gonna have to drink sake instead."

—LEO, THAT 70S SHOW

"Expand my brain, learning juice!"

"Hello, Bureau of Alcohol, Tobacco, and Firearms? I have an alcohol question: Who was in the very first Lite Beer commercial? I say it was Bubba Smith but I have a friend who thinks it was . . . Hello?"

—AL BUNDY, *MARRIED WITH CHILDREN*

"Some drink, drink, drink, drink, drink: do you hear us about? You lazy lout! We want some beer; we want some wine! Pour out the wine, and drink and drink till morning. Pour out the wine for drinking is divine. It is divine. We want some beer; we want some wine. We want some beer; we want some wine."

—STUDENT CHORUS, *THE TALES OF HOFFMAN*

"I have fed purely upon ale; I have eat my ale, drank my ale, and I always sleep upon ale."

—GEORGE FARQUHAR

*McCoy [holding decanter]* Beware of Romulans bearing gifts. Happy Birthday, Jim.

*Kirk*: Thanks. Romulan ale? Why, Bones, you know this stuff is illegal—

*McCoy*: I use it only for medicinal purposes.

—*STAR TREK: THE WRATH OF KHAN*

## POTABLE QUOTABLES

When young Ben Franklin started out as a printer in Philadelphia, he marveled at his coworkers' philosophy that strong beer made a strong laborer. Franklin writes in his *Autobiography*: "My companion at the press drank every day a pint before breakfast, a pint at breakfast with his bread and cheese, a pint between breakfast and dinner, a pint in the afternoon about six o'clock, and another when he had done his day's work."

Since Franklin did not himself drink and did not wish to underwrite other men's habits, he refused to contribute to the weekly beer fund. From that time on, he started turning out printed matter that had a host of errors!

Grudgingly, Franklin started contributing to the beer fund, and wouldn't you know it? His work was free of errors henceforth.

"The best way to die is sit under a tree, eat lots of bologna and salami, drink a case of beer, then blow up."

—ART DONOVAN

"You can search far and wide, you can drink the whole town dry, but you'll never find a beer so brown as the one we drink in our hometown! You can drink your fancy ales, you can drink them by the flagon, but the only brew for the brave and tru-u-u-ue comes from the Green Dragon!"

—MERRY AND PIPPIN, *THE LORD OF THE RINGS: THE RETURN OF THE KING*

*Marcy*: Now can you tell me what a woman's body has to do with selling beer?

*Al*: All right, number one: if it wasn't for beer, there would be at least three people who probably wouldn't be married—me, Jefferson, and probably Lisa Marie Presley. Number two: since men buy beer, advertisers have to cater to what we want. And hold on to your corncob pipe—we like pretty women. Pretty women sell good products, ugly women sell tennis rackets. Pretty women, cars; ugly women, minivans. Pretty women make us buy beer. Ugly women make us drink beer.

—*MARRIED WITH CHILDREN*

"Oh, come on, I love bowling! It's the perfect workout. Six seconds of exercise, drink beer half an hour."

—ROSEANNE, *ROSEANNE*

*Jefferson*: Al, when are we going to stop sipping this beer and start drinking it?

*Griff*: Yeah, all this beer foreplay is making me thirsty.

—*MARRIED WITH CHILDREN*

"We sat and drank with the sun on our shoulders and felt like free men. Hell, we could have been tarring the roof of one of our own houses. We were the lords of all creation. As for Andy, he spent that break hunkered in the shade, a strange little smile on his face, watching us drink his beer."

—RED, *THE SHAWSHANK REDEMPTION*

*Frasier*: Harry, let me get you a beer.

*Harry Moon*: Get a man a beer, he'll drink for five minutes. Teach him where they are, he drinks all day.

—FRASIER

*Raymond*: Do you want me to pour it, Frank?

*Frank Booth*: No I want you to fuck it. Shit, yes, pour the fuckin' beer!

—BLUE VELVET

*Frank Booth*: What kind of beer do you like?

*Jeffrey Beaumont*: Heineken.

*Frank Booth*: [shouting] Heineken? Fuck that shit! Pabst Blue Ribbon!

—BLUE VELVET

# "Milk are for babies, when you get older you drink beer."

—ARNOLD SCHWARZENEGGER, PUMPING IRON

"Heineken? Why it's the finest beer in the world! President Kennedy used to drink it!"

—BUDDUSKY, THE LAST DETAIL

*Coach*: How does a beer sound, Norm?

*Norm*: I don't know Coach. I usually finish 'em before they get a word in.

—CHEERS

"Beer is for breakfast around here, drink or begone."

—BARTENDER DOUG COUGHLIN, COCKTAIL

Barney Gumble: [drinking beer from the tap at Moe's] Uh-oh, my heart just stopped! [pauses] Oh, there it goes.

—THE SIMPSONS

Jeff Dunham: What's your favorite beer?
Bubba J: An open one.
Jeff Dunham: How do you know when you drink too much?
Bubba J: I run out.

—JEFF DUNHAM: ARGUING WITH MYSELF

"Life is too short to drink American beer!"

—THE DEVIL, REAPER

"The best place to drink beer is at home. Or on a river bank, if the fish don't bother you."

—ANONYMOUS

## Chapter 3

# In Vino Veritas

Of all the alcoholic beverages covered in this volume, none has the variety or history of wine—and all from the humble grape! On the glories and subtleties of wine, both the common peasant and the wealthiest noble may agree. White, red, countless shades in between, fruity, dry, sweet, tart, or sparkling, wine offers a tremendous spectrum for all tastes and preferences. Appreciating them all would take a lifetime, and many are happy to spend their lives in the pursuit. Whether you drink wine before a meal, with a meal, after a meal, or simply on its own and for its own sake, wine may be the one drink that stands as the emblem of human civilization.

We don't want to oversell it, though: pour a glass and see for yourself.

"Drink to me only with thine eyes, and I will pledge with mine; or leave a kiss but in the cup and I'll not look for wine."

—BEN JOHNSON

"From wine what sudden friendship springs!"

—JOHN GAY

*Jack*: If they want to drink Merlot, we're drinking Merlot.
  *Miles*: No! If anyone orders Merlot, I'm leaving. I am not drinking any fucking Merlot!

—*SIDEWAYS*

"You just can't remember your lines if you're drinking alcohol. I would say about 95 percent of the time it was grape juice or this fake wine, which was horrible."

—THOMAS HADEN CHURCH, ON FILMING *SIDEWAYS*

"Give me books, fruit, French wine, and fine weather and a little music out of doors, played by somebody I do not know."

—JOHN KEATS

"Other countries drink to get drunk, and this is accepted by everyone; in France, drunkenness is a consequence, never an intention. A drink is felt as the spinning out of a pleasure, not as the necessary cause of an effect which is sought: wine is not only a philter, it is also the leisurely act of drinking."

—ROLAND BARTHES

"Quickly, bring me a beaker of wine, so that I may wet my mind and say something clever."

—ARISTOPHANES

"Beer is made by men, wine by God!"

—Martin Luther

"Wine is a treacherous friend who you must always be on guard for."

—Christian Nevell Bovee

"Wine makes a man more pleased with himself; I do not say that it makes him more pleasing to others."

—Samuel Johnson

"Thanks be to God. Since my leaving the drinking of wine, I do find myself much better, and do mind my business better, and do spend less money, and less time lost in idle company."

—Samuel Pepys

"A bottle of wine contains more philosophy that all the books in the world."

—Louis Pasteur

"You can tell German wine from vinegar by the label."

—Mark Twain

"The world needs water. For every bottle of wine you drink, you contribute to conserving the drinking water reserves."

—Paul Emir Victor

"Wine is wont to show the mind of man."

—Theognis

"I've never been into wine. I'm a beer man. What I like about beer is you basically just drink it and order more. You don't sniff at it, or hold it up to the light and slosh it around, or drone on and on about it, the way people do with wine. Your beer drinker tends to be a straightforward, decent, friendly, down-to-earth person, whereas your serious wine fancier tends to be an insufferable snot."

—Dave Barry

"Who does not love wine, women, and song remains a fool his whole life long."

—Anonymous

"Let us have wine and women, mirth and laughter, / sermons and soda-water the day after."

—LORD BYRON

"Sparkling and bright in liquid light
    Does the wine our goblets gleam in;
    With hue as red as the rosy bed
    Which a bee would choose to dream in."

—CHARLES FENNO HOFFMAN

"Bronze is the mirror of the form; wine, of the heart."

—AESCHYLUS

"Fill every beaker up, my men, pour forth the cheering wine: There's life and strength in every drop—thanksgiving to the vine!"

—ALBERT GORTON GREENE

"I may not here omit those two main plagues and common dotages of human kind, wine and women, which have infatuated and besotted myriads of people; they go commonly together."

—ROBERT BURTON

"With years a richer life begins,
    The spirit mellows:
Ripe age gives tone to violins,
    Wine, and good fellows."

—JOHN TOWNSEND TROWBRIDGE

"I love everything that's old: old friends, old times, old manners, old books, old wine."

—OLIVER GOLDSMITH

"It is better to hide ignorance, but it is hard to do when we relax over wine."

—HERACLITUS

"The wine urges me on, the bewitching wine, which sets even a wise man to singing and to laughing gently and rouses him up to dance and brings forth words which were better unspoken."

—HOMER

"When asked what wine he liked to drink, he replied, 'That which belongs to another.'"

—DIOGENES

"It has become quite a common proverb that in wine there is truth."

—PLINY THE ELDER

"Oh some are fond of Spanish wine, and some are fond of French, and some'll swallow tay [tea] and stuff fit only for a wench."

—JOHN EDWARD MASEFIELD

"Lie soft, sleep hard, drink wine, and eat good cheer."

—THOMAS MIDDLETON

"Wine does but draw forth a man's natural qualities."

—RICHARD BRINSLEY SHERIDAN

"Pour out the wine without restraint or stay, pour not by cups, but by the belly full, pour out to all that will, and sprinkle all the posts and walls with wine, that they may sweat, and drunken be withal."

—EDMUND SPENSER

"Wine gives you liberty, love takes it away."

—WILLIAM WYCHERLEY

"I pray you, do not fall in love with me, for I am falser than vows made in wine."

—ROSALIND, *AS YOU LIKE IT,* WILLIAM SHAKESPEARE

"They are not long, the days of wine and roses: out of a misty dream our path emerges for a while, then closes within a dream."

—ERNEST DOWSON

"Hide our ignorance as we will, an evening of wine soon reveals it."

—HERACLITUS

"A book of verses

underneath the bough,

a jug of wine, a loaf of

bread—and thou."

—EDWARD FITZGERALD

"It is time to get drunk! So as not to be the martyred slaves of Time, get drunk; get drunk without stopping! On wine, on poetry, or on virtue, as you wish."

—CHARLES BAUDELAIRE

"The University of Nebraska says that elderly people that drink beer or wine at least four times a week have the highest bone density. They need it: they're the ones falling down the most."

—JAY LENO

"When the wine goes in, strange things come out."

—JOHANN CHRISTOPH FRIED-
RICH VON SCHILLER

"Wine is bottled poetry."

—ROBERT LOUIS STEVENSON

"Age appears to be best in four things; old wood best to burn, old wine to drink, old friends to trust, and old authors to read."

—FRANCIS BACON

Your
Own
Good
Health

is pledged in a glass of this delicious drink.

Insist on getting it.

PLEASANT
VALLEY
WINE CO.,

Rheims,
New York.

## WATERING SPOTS

Funny how you never see Dionysius and Bacchus together at the same orgy. They must be . . . the same person! Yes, "Bacchus" is the name that the Romans gave to Dionysius, the Greek god of wine, grapes, fertility, theater, beer slides, and wet T-shirt contests. Fans of polysyllabic words refer to a wild party as a "bacchanalia," even though the term originally referred to a secret festival (March 15–16) celebrated by Roman women only. (Woo-hoo!) Evidently the Romans were not content with just one festival of wine and revelry, for they also celebrated the Liberalia (March 17), honoring the Roman god Pater Liber, patron of wine and freedom (and probably free love and free belly shots). Another big party was the "saturnalia," the orgiastic Roman festival honoring Saturn (Dec 17–12). No wonder we wear togas at parties: those Romans knew how to kick it!

"When the wine is in, the wit is out."

—ANONYMOUS

"One of the disadvantages of wine is that it makes a man mistake words for thoughts."

—SAMUEL JOHNSON

"Good friends, go in, and taste some wine with me; and we, like friends, will straightway go together."

—CAESAR, *JULIUS CAESAR*

"This is the great fault of wine; it first trips up the feet: it is a cunning wrestler."

—TITUS MACCIUS PLAUTUS

"Wine gives courage and makes men more apt for passion."

—OVID

"A man who was fond of wine was offered some grapes at dessert after dinner. 'Much obliged,' said he, pushing the plate aside, 'I am not accustomed to take my wine in pills.'"

—JEAN ANTHELME
BRILLAT-SAVARIN

"Dad thinks vengeance is the coolest thing about the Lord. That, and turning water into alcohol."

—CHRISTOPHER TITUS, *TITUS*

## THE DRINKS CABINET

Christian churches have always faced a particular problem when it comes to celebrating the ultimate sacrifice of Jesus: that is, if children are allowed to receive Eucharist, what do we do about the use of wine in the ceremony? Children can't be swilling wine, sanctified or otherwise. To the rescue comes "mustum," a rather unappetizing word for grape juice that has been fermented but a touch. The Roman Catholic Church itself has given the thumbs-up to mustum since the days of Pope Julius I, whose papacy ended in 352 C.E.

"Wine is sunlight, held together by water."

—GALILEO

*Peter Griffin*: Wow, is that really the blood of Christ?
*Preacher*: Yes.
*Peter*: Wow, that guy must've been wasted twenty-four hours a day, huh?

—*FAMILY GUY*

"Sorrow can be alleviated by good sleep, a bath, and a glass of wine."

—THOMAS AQUINAS

"It is a maudlin and indecent verity that comes out through the strength of wine."

—JOSEPH CONRAD

*Don Corleone*: I like to drink wine more than I used to. [*pause*] Anyway, I'm drinking more.
*Michael*: It's good for you, Pop.
*Don Corleone*: Ah, I don't know . . .

—*THE GODFATHER*

"Wine is a turncoat; first a friend and then an enemy."

—HENRY FIELDING

"O thou invisible spirit of wine, if thou hast no name to be known by, let us call thee devil!"

—CASSIO, *OTHELLO* , WILLIAM SHAKESPEARE

"Wine gives a man

nothing . . . it only

puts in motion what

had been locked up in

frost."

—SAMUEL JOHNSON

"You shall have wine enough, my lord, anon."

—SECOND MURDERER, *KING RICHARD III*, WILLIAM SHAKESPEARE

"Ladies, a general welcome from his grace salutes ye all; this night he dedicates to fair content and you: none here, he hopes, in all this noble bevy, has brought with her one care abroad: he would have all as merry as first good company, good wine, good welcome, can make good people."

—GUILDFORD, *KING HENRY VIII*, WILLIAM SHAKESPEARE

"Come, love and health to all; Then I'll sit down. Give me some wine; fill full. I drink to the general joy o' the whole table, And to our dear friend Banquo, whom we miss; would he were here! To all, and him, we thirst, and all to all."

—MACBETH, *MACBETH*, WILLIAM SHAKESPEARE

*Brutus*: Speak no more of her. Give me a bowl of wine. In this I bury all unkindness, Cassius. *Cassius*: My heart is thirsty for that noble pledge. Fill, Lucius, till the wine o'erswell the cup; I cannot drink too much of Brutus' love.

—*JULIUS CAESAR*, WILLIAM SHAKESPEARE

"I am dying, Egypt, dying: Give me some wine, and let me speak a little."

—MARK ANTONY, *ANTONY AND CLEOPATRA*, WILLIAM SHAKESPEARE

Manischewitz isn't. And Christians, that wine you drink at Eucharist? Could be Manischewitz. What? Too good, you think you are for this wine? Oy!

"Champagne is the only wine that leaves a woman beautiful after drinking it."

—MADAME DE POMPADOUR

*Pearl Madison*: You'll have to forgive Mr. Madison today, he's moving kinda slow. His head's hurting like it's the end of the world.

*Guillermo*: You been drinking that cheap ass burgundy, ain't you?

*Pearl Madison*: No comment.

*Bengel*: That stuff's gonna make you go blind, sir.

*Pearl Madison*: Hey, three bucks, two liters. I couldn't pass it up.

—*THE UNITED STATES OF LELAND*

## THE DRINKS CABINET

Even if you're not Jewish, you may have heard derisive cracks and jokes about Manischewitz (the "w" pronounced like a "v") and been too gun-shy to see what all the fuss is about. Manischewitz wine is made from Lambrusco grapes and is sweetened—some say way too much—by either corn syrup (non-Kosher) or cane sugar (Kosher). Originally, producing a wine quickly and locally for Passover produced a bitter wine that had to be sweetened. Terribly expensive,

*Jeremy Usborne*: So, what shall we have to drink, to celebrate?

    *Big Suze*: Well, a Barolo is always nice.

    *Jeremy* [*voiceover*] Shit. Can't ask how much. Restaurant, you have to pretend you're infinitely wealthy for some reason. [*starts looking through the wine list*] OK, flicking, looking. If only I knew the name of any other wine. What's a wine? Is the one Hannibal Lecter drinks real or a joke?

                    —Peep Show

"Great people talk about ideas, average people talk about things, and small people talk about wine."

                    —Fran Lebowitz

"Hamlet's mother, she's the queen
Buys it in the final scene
Drinks a glass of funky wine
Now she's Satan's Valentine!"

              —Soldiers' chant,
              Renaissance Man

## THE DRINKS CABINET

To give your wine more punch, consider whipping up a bowlful of sangria, the wine punch from Spain. Recipes for this popular drink vary widely, so you could concoct something that'll ease you into your siesta after one glass. Of all the recipes in this humble volume, sangria allows for the most experimentation to suit your particular taste: i.e., more sweet, more fruity, or more punch-you-in-the-face alcoholic.

For a summer party or a screening of *Vicky Cristina Barcelona,* consider this approach:

1 bottle red wine

1 bottle sparkling water or ginger ale

¼ cup white sugar

½ cup rum

Juice of fresh lime

Juice of fresh orange

1. Mix in pitcher with ice, adding slices of orange, lemon, pineapple, peaches, you name it.

Now, some recipes put in gin, while others call for brandy, flavored vodka, triple sec, or Cognac. The point here is to give your brew a kick compatible with citrus fruit flavors—and even then, other recipes call for apples in addition to raspberries or blueberries. It's all up to you, amigo.

For an added treat, refrigerate the sangria overnight with the fruit slices soaking in the punch. Mm-mm!

*James Bond*: Pity about your liver, sir. Unusually fine Solera. '51, I believe.

*M*: There is no year for sherry, 007.

*Bond*: I was referring to the original vintage on which the sherry is based, sir. 1851, unmistakable.

—*DIAMONDS ARE FOREVER*

# "Can I get you a drink? I just cracked open a fresh box of wine."

—APRIL RHODES, *GLEE*

---

## WINE OR CHAMPAGNE?

The next time someone asks you which you prefer, wine or Champagne, feel free to inform him or her haughtily that Champagne *is* wine: sparkling wine, in fact. Hence, the inclusion in this chapter of some quotes about bubbly. True lovers of Champagne know three things: genuine Champagne comes only from Champagne, France; the word for this particular sparkling wine is capitalized; and any time is a worthy occasion for Champagne. Cheers!

*Maya*: I—I like to think about the life of wine. How it's a living thing. I like to think about what was going on the year the grapes were growing; how the sun was shining, if it rained. I like to think about all the people who tended and picked the grapes. And if it's an old wine, how many of them must be dead by now. I like how wine continues to evolve, like if I opened a bottle of wine today it would taste different than if I'd opened it on any other day, because a bottle of wine is actually alive. And it's constantly evolving and gaining complexity. That is, until it peaks, like your '61. And then it begins its steady, inevitable decline.

*Miles Raymond*: Hmm.

*Maya*: And it tastes so fucking good.

—*SIDEWAYS*

"Champagne, if you are seeking the truth, is better than a lie detector. It encourages a man to be expansive, even reckless, while lie detectors are only a challenge to tell lies successfully."

—GRAHAM GREENE

"Why do I drink Champagne for breakfast? Doesn't everyone?"

—NOEL COWARD

"My only regret in life is that I didn't drink enough Champagne."

—JOHN MAYNARD KEYNES, DYING WORDS

*René*: May I tell you a little legend, Colonel? It is said that these Champagne glasses were modeled on the bosom of Marie Antoinette.

*Capt. Hans Geering*: They should have modeled them on Helga's bosom. We would have got a bigger drink.

—'ALLO, 'ALLO!

"Too much of anything is bad, but too much Champagne is just right."

—MARK TWAIN

"There comes a time in every woman's life when the only thing that helps is a glass of Champagne."

—BETTE DAVIS

"In victory, you deserve Champagne; in defeat, you need it."

—NAPOLEON BONAPARTE

# "When a man says no to Champagne, he says no to life."

—JULIEN, *THE DEER HUNTER*

"No government could survive without Champagne. Champagne in the throats of our diplomatic people is like oil in the wheels of an engine."

—JOSEPH DARGENT

*"Bat" Masterson*: What are you going to do with all your money?

*Emile Barole*: I'm going to get all the glorious Champagne to drink and all the gorgeous food to eat. Then I'm going to lie down to dream—to dream of more food and more Champagne.

—BAT MASTERSON

"My dear girl, there are some things that just aren't done, such as drinking Dom Perignon '53 above the temperature of 38 degrees Fahrenheit. That's just as bad as listening to the Beatles without earmuffs."

—JAMES BOND, *GOLDFINGER*

"Three be the things I shall never attain: envy, content, and sufficient Champagne."

—DOROTHY PARKER

"Remember gentlemen, it's not just France we are fighting for, it's Champagne!"

—WINSTON CHURCHILL

"I only drink Champagne when I'm happy, and when I'm sad. Sometimes I drink it when I'm alone. When I have company, I consider it obligatory. I trifle with it if I am not hungry and drink it when I am. Otherwise I never touch it—unless I'm thirsty."

—LILY BOLLINGER

"Gentlemen, in the little moment that remains to us between the crisis and the catastrophe, we may as well drink a glass of Champagne."

—PAUL CLAUDEL

"In a perfect world, everyone would have a glass of Champagne every evening."

—WILLIE GLUCKSTERN

"I had taken two finger-bowls of Champagne, and the scene had changed before my eyes into something significant, elemental, and profound."

—F. SCOTT FITZGERALD

"A woman should never be seen eating or drinking, unless it be lobster salad and Champagne, the only true feminine and becoming viands."

—LORD BYRON

"Champagne is the one thing that gives me zest when I feel tired."

—BRIGITTE BARDOT

"Meeting Franklin Roosevelt was like opening your first bottle of Champagne; knowing him was like drinking it."

—WINSTON CHURCHILL

"The feeling of friendship is like that of being comfortably filled with roast beef; love, like being enlivened with Champagne."

—SAMUEL JOHNSON

"The priest has just baptized you a Christian with water; and I baptize you a Frenchman, daring child, with a dewdrop of Champagne on your lips."

—PAUL CLAUDEL

"I'm only a beer teetotaler, not a Champagne teetotaler."

—GEORGE BERNARD SHAW

# "The effervescence of this fresh wine reveals the true brilliance of the French people."

—VOLTAIRE

"I like to start off my day with a glass of Champagne. . . . I like to wind it up with a glass of Champagne, too. To be frank, I also like a glass or two in between. It may not be the universal medicine for every disease, as my friends in Reims and Epernay so often tell me, but it does you less harm than any other liquid."

—CHEF FERNAND POINT

"Champagne for my real friends, real pain for my sham friends."

—FRANCIS BACON [CHARACTER], LOVE IS THE DEVIL: STUDY FOR A PORTRAIT OF FRANCIS BACON

"There are only two occasions when I drink Champagne, and these are: when I have game for dinner and when I haven't."

—S. D. CHURCHILL

"Champagne . . . the wine of kings, the king of wines."

—GUY DE MAUPASSANT

"Champagne is one of the elegant extras in life."

—CHARLES DICKENS

"Champagne! The artillery of pleasure!"

—ROBÈQUE, *BAD GIRLS*

"Burgundy makes you think of silly things, Bordeaux makes you talk about them, and Champagne makes you do them."

—JEAN ANTHELME BRILLAT-SAVARIN

*Zapp Brannigan*: *[after a failed attempt to seduce Leela]* Oh God, I'm pathetic. Sorry. Just go. . . . You want the rest of the sham-PAG-gin?

*Leela*: No, and it's pronounced "sham-PANE."

*Zapp*: *[sobbing]* Oh God, no!

—*FUTURAMA*

## CHAPTER 4

# WHISKEY, GIN, RUM, AND MORE: THAT'S THE SPIRIT!

Surely you've seen a store sign reading "Wine and Spirits" without thinking that in addition to fermented grapes, the retailer sells ghosts, goblins, and things that go bump in the night. (Come to think of it, I go bump in the night when I'm too hammered to get my keys in the door.) The reason why some alcoholic beverages are called "spirits" does indeed trace its origin to medieval thinking that the effects of alcohol could be attributed to demonic possession or influence.

Let us move down the spirits aisle by taking on whiskey, rum, gin, and vodka. We may even have a touch of brandy or sherry—which, technically, is distilled wine, I know, but you don't find brandy cheek by jowl with a fine Chardonnay.

## WHISKEY

All bourbon is whiskey, but not all whiskey is bourbon. Scotch is whiskey made in Scotland, and if you're in Britain and ask for whiskey, they'll bring you Scotch. In America, you have to ask for Scotch to get Scotch. Got it? I don't.

*Will*: Grace, I can see me in a three-way. I can see Karen in a two-way.

*Karen*: Oh, honey, every night with Stan is a three-way: him, me, and Johnnie Walker Black. Just the three of us.

—WILL & GRACE

"Now drink with me deeply of the bourbon, scotch, and rye until such time as we are fighting drunk. Then we shall find, and beat the asses of, the nonbelievers who ruined my feast."

—ALVIS, SEALAB 2021

*Woods*: I'll have a Harvey Wall-banger. Make it a Harvey Oswald.

*Sam Simms*: What's the difference?

*Woods*: Oswald has three shots.

—FIRST KID

"We borrowed golf from Scotland as we borrowed whiskey. Not because it is Scottish, but because it is good."

—HORACE HUTCHINSON

"Bourbon."

—TALLULAH BANKHEAD,
DYING WORDS

"Whiskey is by far the most popular of all remedies that won't cure a cold."

—JERRY VALE

*Scotty*: When are you going to get off that milk diet, lad?
*Chekov*: This is vodka!
*Scotty*: Where I come from, that's soda pop. Now this is a drink for a man.
*Chekov*: Scotch?
*Scotty*: Aye.
*Chekov*: It was invented by a little old lady from Leningrad!

—*STAR TREK*: "THE TROUBLE WITH TRIBBLES"

"I like whiskey. I always did, and that is why I never drink it."

—ROBERT E. LEE

"Never cry over spilt milk. It could've been whiskey."

—"PAPPY" MAVERICK,
*MAVERICK*

"What whiskey will not cure, there is no cure for."

—IRISH PROVERB

"The water was not fit to drink. To make it palatable, we had to add whiskey. By diligent effort, I learned to like it."

—WINSTON CHURCHILL

## THE DRINKS CABINET

The whiskey sour is a drink that contains lemon juice and an added syrup.

> 3 parts Bourbon
>
> 2 parts fresh lemon juice
>
> 1 part gomme syrup (simple syrup with gum arabic added)

1. Shake with ice, strain into tumbler over ice, garnish with Maraschino cherry or orange slice. If you really want a sweet touch, wet the glass rim and dip it into sugar.

A variant cocktail is the Boston sour, which has the unlikely ingredients of powdered sugar and egg white.

> 3 parts blended whiskey
>
> 2 parts fresh lemon juice
>
> 1 teaspoon powdered sugar
>
> 1 egg white

1. Same approach: Shake with ice, strain into tumbler over ice, garnish with Maraschino cherry or orange slice.

Oh, and genius? The egg white should be raw, not cooked.

"I like my whiskey old and my women young."

—ERROL FLYNN

# "I never should have switched from Scotch to martinis."

—HUMPHREY BOGART,
DYING WORDS

*Alan*: [*drinking from Charlie's water bottle*] What the hell is this?
*Charlie*: Bourbon.
*Alan*: You drink bourbon while you work out?
*Charlie*: Gin makes me sweat.

—*TWO AND A HALF MEN*

"God invented the whiskey to keep the Irish from ruling the world."

—ROCK MULLANEY, CROSSFIRE TRAIL

# "I ran out of ice, sir, so I used bourbon."

—"RADAR" O'REILLY, M*A*S*H

"Every Christmas my mom would get a fresh goose for gooseburgers and my dad would whip up his special eggnog out of bourbon and ice cubes."

—PHILIP FRY, FUTURAMA

"An Irishman is lined with copper, and the beer corrodes it. But whiskey polishes the copper and is the saving of him."

—MARK TWAIN

## THE DRINKS CABINET

Two iconic cocktails—the Rob Roy and the Manhattan—are strikingly similar. Named after a famous Scotsman, the Rob Roy contains (you guessed it) Scotch, while the Manhattan may be made with rye, Canadian whiskey, or bourbon.

2 ounces Scotch whiskey (Rob Roy) or Canadian whiskey (Manhattan)

1 ounce sweet vermouth

Dash of Angostura bitters

1. Shake with ice, strain over ice or into a chilled glass, garnish with a maraschino cherry.

A "dry Rob Roy" uses dry vermouth, and a "perfect Rob Roy" is equal parts sweet and dry and vermouth: these two versions get a lemon garnish instead of a cherry.

If you drink too many Rob Roys, you will, like a good Scotsman, start brawling; if you drink too many Manhattans, you will, like a good New Yorker, have your lawyer threaten to sue.

"A little honey a day keeps the bourbon away."

—MIKE HAMMER, I, THE JURY

"Champagne's funny stuff. I'm used to whiskey. Whiskey is a slap on the back, and Champagne's heavy mist before my eyes."

—MACAULEY CONNOR, *THE PHILADELPHIA STORY*

"Are you desirable? Are you irresistible? Maybe if you drank bourbon with me, it would help. Maybe if you kissed me and I could taste the sting in your mouth it would help—if you drank bourbon with me naked. If you smelled of bourbon as you fucked me, it would help. It would increase my esteem for you. If you poured bourbon onto your naked body and said to me, 'Drink this.' If you spread your legs and you had bourbon dripping from your breasts and your pussy and said 'Drink here' then I could fall in love with you. Because then I would have a purpose. To clean you up and that, that would prove that I'm worth something. I'd lick you clean so that you could go away and fuck someone else."

—BEN SANDERSON, *LEAVING LAS VEGAS*

"When an alibi is full of bourbon, sir, it can't stand up."

—GUY HAINES, *STRANGERS ON A TRAIN*

"One man I know suffers so much he has to take a medication called bourbon, even that doesn't help very much because then he can hear paint dry."

—MORK, *MORK & MINDY*

"Me? I'll take bourbon. It kills you slower, but a lot more pleasant like."

—JACK THORNTON, *THE CALL OF THE WILD*

"Shut up! It's 'Daddy,' you shithead! Where's my bourbon? Can't you fucking remember anything?"

—FRANK BOOTH, AFTER BEING ADDRESSED BY HIS REAL NAME, *BLUE VELVET*

"I'm running low. I'd like to make it to a state store before they all shut their doors forever. God, there's a terrible thought. A world where a gentleman can't buy a bottle of bourbon."

—ANDREW MAXWELL, *DIARY OF THE DEAD*

"Generally I recommend my men stay away from vodka, and stick with scotch and bourbon."

—NICK FRESCIA,
TEQUILA SUNRISE

"Nothing is so musical as the sound of pouring bourbon for the first drink on a Sunday morning. Not Bach or Schubert or any of those masters."

—CARSON MCCULLERS

*Mrs. Gideon*: Ohhh! I hope that wasn't whiskey you were drinking.
*Cuthbert J. Twillie (W.C. Fields)*: Ah, no, dear, just a little sheep dip. Panacea for all stomach ailments.

—MY LITTLE CHICKADEE

*Mary Kate Danaher*: Could you use a little water in your whiskey?
*Michaleen Flynn*: When I drink whiskey, I drink whiskey; and when I drink water, I drink water.

—THE QUIET MAN

*Paladin*: Oh, are the Irish so bad?
*Renato Donatello*: What kind of savages would drink whiskey made from potatoes?

—HAVE GUN—WILL TRAVEL

"You know, I never learned how to sip a drink. When I was very little, every evening before supper my father would pour a shot glass full of whiskey, mumble a prayer, and down it went! I thought that was the way you drank."

—HECKY BROWN, THE FRONT

"Laddie, I was drinking scotch a hundred years before you were born. And I can tell you that whatever this is, it is definitely not scotch."

—ENGINEER MONTGOMERY SCOTT, AFTER DATA SERVES HIM "SYNTHEHOL," STAR TREK: THE NEXT GENERATION

"I take a whiskey drink, I take a coffee drink, and when I have to pee, I use the kitchen sink. I sing the song that reminds me I'm a urinating guy."

—HOMER SIMPSON, SINGING TO TUNE OF CHUMBAWUMBA'S "TUBTHUMPING," THE SIMPSONS

*Marge*: Bart, are you drinking whiskey?
*Bart*: I'm troubled!

—THE SIMPSONS MOVIE

## THE DRINKS CABINET

The word "bourbon" is French, but bourbon is whiskey from America. (It's named after Bourbon County, Kentucky.) American whiskey doesn't exceed 80 percent alcohol per volume.

Rye whiskey is made from rye, which is a type of grass closely related to wheat and barley. Both corn whiskey and bourbon are made from corn, but whereas bourbon has at least 51 percent corn, corn whiskey has at least 80 percent.

Bourbon cannot be artificially flavored or colored after it's filtered.

Tennessee whiskey (the most famous being Jack Daniel's) is made using a special filtering process in which the liquid passes through a column of maple charcoal.

Straight whiskey refers to whiskey that is aged for more than two years, is no more than 80 percent alcohol by volume, and is derived from less than 51 percent of any kind of grain.

Blended whiskey is what it sounds like: a blend of different single-malt whiskeys.

Which brings us to malting: a process applied to grains when making alcohol. Single-malt whiskey contains one grain (usually barley) that has undergone the malting process and has been distilled at one location.

"Captain, down around where I come from we dearly love our whiskey. But we don't drink with another man unless we respect him."

—SFC TOLLIVER, *ATTACK*

*Cartman*: I don't believe it. She's using the Mel Gibson defense!

*Miss Stevenson*: I am a perfectly good person, but when I drink, the alcohol makes me say and do things I wouldn't normally do.

*Police Sergeant*: Well, that explains it.

*Policeman #1*: Do we still press charges?

*Police Sergeant*: Who are we gonna convict? Johnnie Walker?

—*SOUTH PARK*

"A torchlight procession marching down your throat."

—JOHN LOUIS O'SULLIVAN,
DESCRIBING WHISKEY

*Nessa Holt*: OK, here's to all those Cosmo-drinking, *Cosmo*-reading airheads.

*Nessa, Samantha*: [*clinking glasses*] Screw 'em.

—*LAS VEGAS*

"According to *The Hitchhiker's Guide to the Galaxy*, the best drink in the known universe is the Pan-Galactic Gargle Blaster. It has the effect of having your brains smashed out with a slice of lemon . . . wrapped around a large gold brick."

—THE BOOK, *THE HITCHHIKER'S GUIDE TO THE GALAXY*

# "The martini: the only American invention as perfect as the sonnet."

—H. L. MENCKEN

*Tony D'Annunzio*: Another Rob Roy, Bishop?

*Bishop*: You never ask a Navy man if he'll have another drink, because it's nobody's goddamned business how much he's had already.

*Judge Smalls*: Wrong, you're drinking too much, your Excellency.

*Bishop*: Excellency, fiddle sticks. My name's Fred and I'm a man, same as you.

—*CADDYSHACK*

"If when you say 'whiskey' you mean the devil's brew, the poison scourge, the bloody monster that defiles innocence, dethrones reason . . . then I am certainly against it. But, if when you say 'whiskey' you mean the oil of conversation, the philosophic wine . . . the drink that enables a man to magnify his joy . . . then I am certainly for it. This is my stand. I will not retreat from it. I will not compromise."

—NOAH SWEAT

"I died in 1938. For exercise, we drank sloe gin and smoked Lucky Strikes."

—DAISY ADAIR, *DEAD LIKE ME*

*Jane Deaux*: What's that? It smells like you're frying vomit!

*Dharma*: Close. I'm making a great big pot of Haggis.

*Jane*: What have you been drinking?

*Dharma*: Scotch! Which was invented by the great Scotsman Angus McBarf when his wife told him what was for dinner.

—*DHARMA & GREG*


*Kitty*: Come Edward, there's someone I'd like you to meet.

*Edward*: I hope his name is Johnnie Walker.

*Kitty*: It's the archbishop.

*Edward*: I hope it's Archbishop Johnnie Walker.

—*DHARMA & GREG*


**THE DRINKS CABINET**

Second to the "hair of the dog" theory (i.e., drinking alcohol the morning after helps relieve a hangover) is the "hot toddy" theory, which suggests that spiked tea or cider helps relieve the symptoms of a head cold or the flu.

Regardless of its scientific merits, or lack thereof, the hot toddy theory has cheered many a miserable patient through the centuries, and if nothing else, may help induce a welcome nap.

Put a shot of whiskey into a mug, and add boiling water. Stir in a spoonful of honey and, if desired, add two cloves and a cinnamon stick. Let the drink sit for a few minutes, and drink with the cloves and cinnamon stick in, or out.

You could also add the whiskey to mulled cider and enjoy a hot toddy on a cold night when you're not feeling sick at all. You might say that whether you're under the weather or not, the forecast can always call for hot toddies.

---

# GIN

There are some spirits that are absolutely essential to one's bar stock, gin topping the list. To accommodate a variety of tastes, one should have distilled gin (the traditional neutral spirit) and compound gin (distilled gin with added flavoring). Without gin, there would be no martinis, and that's a scenario too troubling to contemplate sober.


"We shall drink to our partnership. Do you like gin? It is my only weakness."

—DR. PRETORIUS, *BRIDE OF FRANKENSTEIN*

"I like to drink martinis. Two at the most. Three I'm under the table, four I'm under the host."

—DOROTHY PARKER

"One gin and tonic, size large, sir, for the use of."

—JOHNNY HOLLIS, *JOHNNY IN THE CLOUDS*

"Zen martini: A martini with no vermouth at all. And no gin, either."

—P. J. O'ROURKE

"The three-martini lunch is the epitome of American efficiency. Where else can you get an earful, a bellyful and a snootful at the same time?"

—GERALD FORD

"I am prepared to believe that a dry martini slightly impairs the palate, but think what it does for the soul."

—ALEC WAUGH

"It's true love because if he said quit drinking martinis but I kept on drinking them and the next morning I couldn't get out of bed, he wouldn't tell me he told me."

—JUDITH VIORST

"If it wasn't for the olives in his martinis, he'd starve to death!"

—MILTON BERLE

"New York is the greatest city in the world for lunch: That's the gregarious time. And when that first martini hits the liver like a silver bullet, there is a sigh of contentment that can be heard in Dubuque."

—WILLIAM EMERSON JR.

# "Happiness is finding two olives in your martini when you're hungry."

—Johnny Carson

"Gin is an alcoholic beverage, which, if your mommy's strong genes are any indication, you'll eventually learn to love as it slowly destroys a giant portion of your adult life."

—Dr. Cox, *Scrubs*

*Frank*: Haven't you two anything better to do when you're off duty than to lie around and swill gin?
*Hawkeye*: Swill gin? Sir, I have sipped, lapped and taken gin intravenously, but I have never swilled!

—*M\*A\*S\*H*

*Margaret*: [*pouring another drink*] It's funny how you only get to know people after they're gone. I feel real close to you right now.
*Henry Blake*: Yeah, sure. Uh, that, uh, scotch you just poured is rye.
*Margaret*: That's OK. The Champagne I just had was gin.

—*M\*A\*S\*H*

"Of all the gin joints, in all the towns, in all the world . . . she walks into mine."

—Rick Blaine, *Casablanca*

"Not her! Gin was mother's milk to her. Besides, he poured so much down his own throat, he knew the good of it."

—Eliza Doolittle,
*My Fair Lady*

## THE DRINKS CABINET
Think of a Tom Collins as lemonade for grownups. This bartending staple is simple, sweet, and strikes a nice middle ground between fruity girl drinks and hard-ass men's drinks that taste like wood.

As always, use quality gin, fresh juices, and your own simple syrup, which is basically sugar dissolved in water.

> 2 parts gin
>
> 1 part lemon juice
>
> Drizzle of simple syrup

1. Mix, and add carbonated water to taste
2. Serve over ice in a Tom Collins glass with a lemon slice or maraschino cherry as a garnish.

The "Collins" here refers to the sweet lemon flavor: feel free to experiment and substitute for the gin. The most popular substitute is vodka, giving you a Vodka Collins. Why not try rum (Ron Collins), bourbon (John Collins), or tequila (Juan Collins)?

You could also try to come up with a cocktail that deserves the name Joan Collins, after the trashy British actress: the only requirement would be that, like its namesake, the drink goes down easily.

"A good heavy book holds you down. It's an anchor that keeps you from getting up and having another gin and tonic."

—ROY BLOUNT JR.

"The proper union of gin and vermouth is a great and sudden glory; it is one of the happiest marriages on earth, and one of the shortest lived."

—BERNARD DEVOTO

"No. There are limits. I mean, a man can put up with only so much without he descends a rung or two on the old evolutionary ladder, which is up your line. Now, I will hold your hand when it's dark and you're afraid of the boogeyman and I will tote your gin bottles out after midnight so no one can see but I will not light your cigarette. And that, as they say, is that."

—GEORGE, *WHO'S AFRAID OF VIRGINIA WOOLF?*

"Gin! I knew there was something wrong with that guy. I never met a gin drinker yet that you could trust."

—PARNELL MCCARTHY, *ANATOMY OF A MURDER*

"An Englishman's gin bottle is his castle!"

—HORACE RUMPOLE, *RUMPOLE OF THE BAILEY*

"Give me a tall glass of warm gin with a human hair in it."

—REX O'HERLIHAN,
RUSTLER'S RHAPSODY

"People I can do without. This is my list: guys in their fifties named 'Skip.' Anyone who pays for vaginal jelly with an Exxon credit card. . . . A cross-eyed nun with a bullwhip and a bottle of gin!"

—GEORGE CARLIN

*President Bartlet*: Can I tell you what's messed up about James Bond?
*Charlie Young*: Nothing.
*President Bartlet*: "Shaken, not stirred" will get you cold water with a dash of gin and dry vermouth. The reason you stir it with a special spoon is so not to chip the ice. James is ordering a weak martini and being snooty about it.

—THE WEST WING

"Oh, man. Don't you know only squares drink gin martinis with olives?"

—CHANCE WAYNE,
SWEET BIRD OF YOUTH

"Tess's mom has a strict rule that we can't do anything on Christmas Day that Jesus didn't do. Apparently Jesus drank a pitcher of martinis and hit on the caterer."

—HENRY, STARK RAVING MAD

"I hope you won't mind waiting while I remove these wet things and slip into a dry martini."

—BUGS BUNNY (IMITATING
GROUCHO MARX), SLICK HARE

"They say a martini is like a woman's breast: one ain't enough and three is too many."

—GAIL, *THE PARALLAX VIEW*

"He knows just how I like my martini: full of alcohol."

—HOMER SIMPSON, *THE SIMPSONS*

"I'd like a dry martini, Mr. Quoc. A very dry martini. A very dry, arid, barren, desiccated, veritable dustbowl of a martini. I want a martini that could be declared a disaster area. Mix me just such a martini."

—"HAWKEYE" PIERCE, *M*A*S*H*

"You pour six jiggers of gin, and you drink it while staring at a picture of Lorenzo Schwartz, the inventor of Vermouth."

—"HAWKEYE" PIERCE ON MAKING THE PERFECT MARTINI, *M*A*S*H*

## VODKA

Vodka is the only thing that makes potatoes palatable, and without vodka, Russia would have won the Cold War. The word itself comes from the Slavic term for "water," or "voda." Somehow the "k" sound gives it more of a kick, doncha think?

"I'll stick with gin. Champagne is just ginger ale that knows somebody."

—"HAWKEYE" PIERCE, *M*A*S*H*

*Captain Pike*: What the devil are you putting in there, ice?

*Dr. Boyce*: Who wants a warm martini?

*Captain Pike*: What makes you think I need one?

*Dr. Boyce*: Sometimes a man will tell his bartender things he'll never tell his doctor.

—*STAR TREK: THE MENAGERIE*, PART 1

"You say potato, I say vodka."

—KAREN, *WILL & GRACE*

"Vodka, that's an alcohol rub from the inside."

—LARRY, *THE FACTS OF LIFE*

## THE DRINKS CABINET

You can't get much simpler than the screwdriver: vodka and orange juice. But simplicity affords a wide berth for experimentation.

Adventurous drinkers use vodka to spike a wide variety of orange-flavored drinks and call them "screwdrivers": e.g., vodka and orange Gatorade, vodka and Sunny Delight, vodka and orange soda, vodka and Orangina (aka a "Hi-Fi"), vodka and Tang. As high school as those concoctions sound, there's no accounting for taste. If you like it, you like it.

Vodka maker Absolut manufactures a "Mandarin" variety that combines the flavors of orange and mandarin if you wish to punch up the flavor further. You could also experiment by using some other citrus-flavored vodka or combining vodka and orange juice with some other fruit-based liqueur or nonalcoholic fruit juice.

Note that if you top off a screwdriver with the herbal liqueur Galliano, you have a Harvey Wallbanger. A screwdriver with a splash of dark rum gives you a brass monkey. And if you substitute Champagne for the vodka— i.e., Champagne and orange juice—you get a mimosa.

Bear in mind that using top-shelf vodka and freshly squeezed orange juice will give you a drink superior to one using bargain-basement vodka and something stirred together from powder or frozen concentrate. Good ingredients yield good results.

"Money, like vodka, turns a person into an eccentric."

—ANTON CHEKHOV

"The relationship between a Russian and a bottle of vodka is almost mystical."

—RICHARD OWEN

"Vodka is tasteless going down, but it is memorable coming up."

—GARRISON KEILLOR

"Just because there is vodka in my freezer it doesn't mean I have to drink it. Wait, yes it does."

—EMERSON COD, *PUSHING DAISIES*

## THE DRINKS CABINET

The cosmopolitan is a cocktail whose very name means "sophistication," albeit with a connotation of "female sophistication" because of its sweet and fruity flavor and the fact that the drink's resurgence is credited to Carrie and the girls on *Sex and the City*.

To make a superior cosmopolitan, use top-shelf vodka and fresh cranberry juice: that "juice" you buy at the supermarket is often jacked up with sugars. If you make your own cranberry juice—i.e., by buying cranberries and liquefying them in your blender or juicer—the results are likely to taste bitter, so add some fresh lemon, fresh apple juice, or sugar to taste.

| |
|---|
| 6 ounces vodka |
| 1 shot Cointreau |
| 1 shot fresh lime juice |
| 4½ ounces cranberry juice |

Serve in a cocktail class (aka martini glass) with a lime wedge or lemon slice. You can also use lemon vodka instead of regular vodka or, triple sec instead of Cointreau. The cranberry juice is there for color, not to dilute the alcohol.

And note that a cocktail of just vodka and cranberry juice is called a Cape Codder (Cape Cod in Massachusetts being a famous producer of cranberries).

"What you really want after a fight is whiskey 'cause it mellows you out.

If you want to get mean you drink gin. Vodka if you want to zone out and you save tequila for when you want to get crazy."

—T. K. POOLE, *THE LUCKY ONES*

*Tom*: Are you on the booze again?

*Diana*: Sure am, Ollie.

*Tom*: What is it this time?

*Diana*: Wod-ka. I've decided to drink a bottle of vodka every morning until I die.

*Tom*: Which will be about next Wednesday morning.

*Diana*: With a bit of luck.

—*WAITING FOR GOD*

"As the only woman, I was able to sit with the officers in front, with a glass of vodka in one hand and a cucumber in the other. That's how I went to my first war."

—ASNE SEIERSTAD

"I believe that if life gives you lemons, you should make lemonade. . . . And try to find somebody whose life has given them vodka, and have a party."

—RON WHITE

"I have a punishing workout regimen. Every day I do three minutes on a treadmill, then I lie down, drink a glass of vodka, and smoke a cigarette."

—ANTHONY HOPKINS

**THE DRINKS CABINET**
When the cocktail the Black Russian was invented (1949), the Russians were our former allies, our emerging enemies, and the subject of mystery and suspicion—sounds like a drinking buddy for sure.

7½ ounces vodka

3 ounces Kahlúa or other coffee liqueur

1. Pour the vodka over ice in an Old Fashioned glass, then add liqueur. Stir.
2. Add a dash of lemon juice to the Black Russian for a Black Magic.

Substitute a Tom Collins glass and add Coke or other cola to the top, and you have a Tall Black Russian.

(Why not a Rasputin? It's a cooler name.) Substitute Guinness for the cola, and you get an Irish Russian. Substitute ginger ale for the cola, and you get a Brown Russian.

Either way, your eyes will be Russian red in no time.

# RUM

A testimony to the adult sweet tooth, rum is liquor distilled from molasses and the juice of sugarcane. Most often associated with pirates, bootleggers, and equatorial Edens, rum is used both in mixed drinks (usually light rum) and drunk straight (usually darker rum). And did I mention you can cook with it, too? An absence of rules governing the production of rum has, happily, given the world dozens of varieties of rum, of varying colors, flavors, and salutary effects.

"RUM, noun. Generically, fiery liquors that produce madness in total abstainers."

—AMBROSE BIERCE

"Let us candidly admit that there are shameful blemishes on the American past, of which the worst by far is rum. Nevertheless, we have improved man's lot and enriched his civilization with rye, bourbon, and the martini cocktail. In all history has any other nation done so much?"

—BERNARD DEVOTO

"Among the expected glories of the Constitution, next to the abolition of Slavery was that of Rum."

—GEORGE CLYMER

*Capt. Hornblower*: Aside from water, I shall need 200 bullocks, 500 pigs, 100 quintals of salt, 40 tons of flour, 10 tons of sugar, 5 tons of tobacco, 1 ton of coffee, the juice of 40,000 limes and, um, are there any wines to be had here?

*Hernandez*: We drink a spirit distilled from molasses which you probably do not know. We call it rum. Will that do?

*Capt. Hornblower*: Ha-hmm. Well, if there's nothing better that will have to do. One hundred barrels.

—*CAPTAIN HORATIO HORN-BLOWER R.N.*

"Fifteen men on a dead man's chest
  YO HO HO and a bottle of rum
  Drink and the devil have done for the rest
  YO HO HO and a bottle of rum."

—ROBERT LOUIS STEVENSON, *TREASURE ISLAND*

"Eye of rabbit, harp string hum, turn this water into *rum*."

—SEAMUS FINNIGAN, *HARRY POTTER AND THE SORCERER'S STONE*

"My body is like a *rum* chocolate soufflé: if I don't warm it up right, it doesn't rise."

—KURT HUMMEL, *GLEE*

"Yes, in the old days, when he used to run *rum* out of Mexico and I was on the other side. We used to swap shots between drinks, or drinks between shots, whichever you like."

—PHILIP MARLOWE, *THE BIG SLEEP*

"Don't talk to me about naval tradition! It's nothing but rum, sodomy, and the lash."

—WINSTON CHURCHILL (APOCRYPHAL)

"The first time I played the Masters, I was so nervous I drank a bottle of rum before I teed off. I shot the happiest 83 of my life."

—CHI CHI RODRIGUEZ

## THE DRINKS CABINET

If your party invitation list includes hipsters, faux-hemians, and fat dudes in Hawaiian shirts, be prepared to make that staple of Polynesian "tiki culture," the mai tai: a rum cocktail evoking the post–World War II glorification of the South Pacific.

You should also be prepared for a dose of mai tai elitism, as there is no one definitive recipe for the drink. The fat dude in the Hawaiian shirt may lecture you that the mai tai was invented in 1944 in a California bar called Trader Vic's, and that the "Vic" mai tai is the one and only *true* tai:

> 2 ounces 17-year-old J. Wray & Nephew Rum, over shaved ice
>
> Juice of one fresh lime
>
> ½ ounce Holland DeKuyper Orange Curaçao
>
> ¼ ounce Trader Vic's Rock Candy Syrup
>
> ½ ounce French Garnier Orgeat Syrup

1. Shake vigorously, and add a sprig of fresh mint as a garnish.

An acceptable substitute for "Rock Candy Syrup" is homemade simple syrup (sugar dissolved in water). Other recipes add pineapple juice or triple sec. Still other recipes combine white rum and dark rum. You may also garnish the mai tai with a lime wedge, a pineapple wedge, and as many umbrellas and tiki swizzle sticks as you desire. Hell, insert a lit sparkler if you got 'em. This drink is all about color, sweetness, flourish, and fun.

> "Ha! See where the wild-blazing Grog-shop appears,
>
> As the red waves of wretchedness swell;
>
> How it burns on the edge of tempestuous years—
>
> The horrible Light-house of Hell!"
>
> —"THE RUM-HOLE," MCDONALD CLARKE

> "The only way that I could figure they could improve on Coca-Cola, one of life's most delightful elixirs, which studies prove will heal the sick and occasionally raise the dead, is to put rum or bourbon in it."
>
> —LEWIS GRIZZARD

> "If it be the design of Providence to extirpate these savages in order to make room for the cultivation of the earth, it seems not improbably that rum may be the appointed means."
>
> —BENJAMIN FRANKLIN

## THE DRINKS CABINET

Now, now, no need to worry: drinking a zombie will not turn you into one. That only happens when you have more than two in the course of an evening. Along with its cousin the Long Island Iced Tea, the zombie is notorious for packing an alcoholic punch under a veneer of sweet fruitiness:

> 1 part white rum
>
> 1 part golden rum
>
> 1 part dark rum
>
> 1 part apricot brandy
>
> 1 part pineapple juice
>
> 1 part papaya juice
>
> ½ part 151-proof rum
>
> Dash of grenadine or simple syrup

1. Mix all the ingredients in a shaker with ice and serve straight up. You could also mix all ingredients except the 151-proof rum, pour into a glass, and top with the high-proof rum. Some folks who favor presentation insist on lighting this drink on fire: just keep the matches away from the drinker's breath.

"If you keep drinking rum, the world will soon be quit of a very dirty scoundrel."

—ROBERT LOUIS STEVENSON

"It was understood that nothing of a tender nature could possibly be confided to old Barley, by reason of his being totally unequal to the consideration of any subject more psychological than gout, rum, and purser's stores."

—CHARLES DICKENS

"I pity them greatly, but I must be mum, for how could we do without sugar and rum?"

—WILLIAM COWPER

"The party whose antecedents are rum, Romanism, and rebellion."

—SAMUEL DICKINSON BURCHARD, REFERRING TO THE DEMOCRATIC PARTY

## POTABLE QUOTABLES

The next time you are at your British Explorer's Club, sipping brandy by the hearth in an oak-paneled room, and one of your stout, mutton-chopped colleagues chortles about "having a rum go," know that he is not referring to making a run for some Captain Morgan's. In Brit-speak, a "rum go" is an odd or unexpected experience. Oddly, the adjective "rum" was used to connote excellence; over time, it took on the meaning of peculiar. Talk about a rum etymology, eh? O-haw! Yes! Quite! Harrumph!

"Jack, I am not going to make any excuses. Yes, Little Jack wouldn't stop crying so I gave him some hugs and I let him watch TV. I went to answer the phone, I was gone for a second, I came back, he let himself out of the playpen, he put on *Scarface*, and he glued his hands to the *rum* bottle. OK? That's it."

—GREG FOCKER, *MEET THE FOCKERS*

"You know what? We all love Yoo-Hoo, especially Yoo-Hoo with a little *rum*."

—SONNY, *BIG DADDY*

"I've been drinking *rum* and coke since before he was born, he can go fuck himself."

—SUZETTE, *THE BANGER SISTERS*

## BRANDY

The favored drink of great leaders such as Ulysses S. Grant and Captain James T. Kirk, brandy is distilled wine typically served as an after-dinner *digestif*. Cognac is a type of brandy, produced exclusively in an area in France by the same name. Brandy is usually served in a bowl-like glass called a snifter and, some say, tastes best beside a roaring fire.

"Glass of brandy and water! That is the current but not the appropriate name: ask for a glass of liquid fire and distilled damnation."

—ROBERT HALL

"Crazed with avarice, lust and rum, New York, thy name's Delirium."

—BYRON R. NEWTON

"An American monkey after getting drunk on brandy would never touch it again, and thus is much wiser than most men."

—CHARLES DARWIN

"Claret is the liquor for boys, port for men; but he who aspires to be a hero must drink brandy."

—SAMUEL JOHNSON

"When I am an old woman I shall wear purple, with a red hat which doesn't go and doesn't suit me, And I shall spend my pension on brandy and summer gloves, And satin sandals, and say we've no money for butter."

—JENNY JOSEPH

"She's crazier than a rat in a brandy keg!"

—ELOISE DALTON, *EYES OF FIRE*

"We all drew on the comfort which is given out by the major works of Mozart, which is as real and material as the warmth given up by a glass of brandy."

—REBECCA WEST

"When I see a merchant over-polite to his customers, begging them to taste a little brandy and throwing half his goods on the counter—thinks I, that man has an axe to grind."

—CHARLES MINER

## THE DRINKS CABINET

The B&B is one of those no-brainer cocktails that's exceptionally hard to mess up: equal parts brandy and Bénédictine. Pour over ice, stir, drink. Done.

Bénédictine is an herbal liqueur first made by (you guessed it) monks. The recipe calls for twenty-seven herbs and plants and probably some whispered mumbo-jumbo, too. When you buy a bottle of Bénédictine, note the "D.O.M." on the label, which stands not for "Dominican Order of Monks" but for the Latin phrase "Deo Optimo Maximo," or "For our best, greatest God." So if the gods on Olympus drink ambrosia, the Lord God must order a B&B when He's tired of listening to your prayers. My guess is that He makes it a double.

## THE DRINKS CABINET

The Brandy Alexander is for the taste buds that crave something smooth, creamy, chocolaty, and potent—kind of like an alcoholic Milky Way bar.

Legend has it that in the early 1970s, when John Lennon went on a drunken journey into the dark heart of Los Angeles with Harry Nilsson, the former Beatle favored this drink—I mean, *really* favored it. (Unlike you, Lennon probably had a limo to drive him home.)

1 part Cognac

1 part dark crème de cacao

1 part half-and-half, or better, fresh cream

1. Shake in a mixer with ice cubes, strain into a cocktail (martini) glass, and garnish with fresh nutmeg or chocolate.

And enjoy! Although in the name of all that is holy, don't down half a dozen of these on karaoke night and then tackle "Imagine."

"BRANDY, n. A cordial composed of one part thunder-and-lightning, one part remorse, two parts bloody murder, one part death-hell-and-the-grave and four parts clarified Satan."

—AMBROSE BIERCE

*Roger*: I had a wonderful night's rest. You know the trouble I have sleeping? Well, I've solved it. Just before you go to bed you put three tranquilizers in a jigger of brandy and you drink it. You still can't sleep but you're so relaxed that you don't worry about it. It was exhilarating.

*Philip Shayne*: Fancy that. And some people just go to sleep and never know what they're missing.

—*THAT TOUCH OF MINK*

*Bev Harris*: I think we should all have some tea . . . and then pour large amounts of brandy into it.

*Roseanne*: Darlene, would you put on some water, and then . . . bring the brandy down from your room.

*Darlene*: Very funny. Don't you think if I had brandy in my room, I'd spend more time at home?

—*ROSEANNE*

"I told you. The moment you start drinking that Bosnian brandy, the devil's sitting in the corner, just laughing."

—DUCK, *THE HUNTING PARTY*

*Ernie Malone*: What are you girls made of? What was that?

    *Lorelei Lee*: Just equal parts of scotch, vodka, brandy, and gin.

—Gentlemen Prefer Blondes

"Teddy, I'm a Scotch drinker, you know that. I just have the occasional brandy when I'm not drinking."

—Jim Naboth, The Squeeze

*Calypso*: Brandy's the very best drink in the world. If you drink enough your toes get curled.

    *Dr. Walters*: Calypso, statistics show that if the level of alcohol in the blood exceeds one half of one percent, the blood pressure is affected, a cerebral condition occurs, and then . . . you're cockeyed. [*takes a drink of liquor, nods approvingly, then exhales*] And maybe that's the way it should be.

—Brute Force

"If this fellow had had his way with me, I don't suppose I'd ever have had another brandy and soda. That's a dismal thought, isn't it? You know it hadn't occurred to me before, but this brandy-and-soda business put it into my mind, that being dead must be rather like living in America, you know? It's a dry state."

—Lord Montague,
The Unholy Night

## THE DRINKS CABINET

Ultra-suave actor Cary Grant changed his name from Archibald Leach—for obvious reasons. Some names just sound better on the lips. Similarly, you sound cooler ordering a stinger than you would ordering a "hanky-panky" or an "angel's tit."

> 3 parts brandy
>
> 1 part white crème de menthe

1. Mix in a shaker and strain into a cocktail glass, or serve over ice.

Substitute green crème de menthe for white and you get a Green Hornet. You also get a grosser mess if you have too many and have to hurl. Just saying.

*Lila*: Chris? Sit down. [*Christian comes over and sits down, as she pours him a brandy.*] Drink that. [*Christian takes a small sip.*] Toss it: that way, it's medicinal.

[*Christian knocks back the drink.*] Good! It's vital for a man to have a couple of slugs in him before discussing heartache. I think Hemingway told me that.

*Christian*: You knew Ernest Hemingway?

*Lila*: Margaux, actually. But beauties don't always escape tragedy.

—*LATTER DAYS*

"If you want a drink, sir—compliments Henry Blake—brandy, scotch, vodka. And for your convenience, all in the same bottle."

—"RADAR" O'REILLY, M*A*S*H

"I never drink anything stronger than gin before breakfast."

—W. C. FIELDS

"The Indians gave up the land of their own free will, and for it received brass kettles, blankets, guns, shirts, flints, tobacco, rum and many trinkets in which their simple hearts delighted."

—PATRICK GORDON

"There's naught, no doubt, so much the spirit calms as rum and true religion."

—LORD BYRON

## THE DRINKS CABINET

A sweet cocktail with origins in the early twentieth century, the sidecar has a retro sophistication. Its ingredients are basic enough: brandy (or Cognac), Cointreau, and lemon juice. How could you mess that up? Easy: age and quality of ingredients.

Cognac is graded according to the number of years it spends stored in the cask: VS, or "Very Special" (two years); VSOP, or "Very Special Old Pale" (four years); and XO, or "Extra Old" (at least six, preferably fifteen or more). Brandy, too, is similarly graded, although with slight variation in numbers of years spent in cask.

Instead of Cointreau, you may use Grand Marnier or another type of triple sec. And natch, the lemon juice should be fresh-squeezed, no seeds falling into the glass.

Now, depending on your age, palette, and whether or not you think cocktails should taste like candy bars, you may want to opt out of a traditional sidecar element: cane sugar around the rim. Be specific, when ordering.

1 part Cognac (or brandy)

1 part Cointreau

1 part lemon juice

Lemon rind garnish (optional)

Sugared rim (optional)

1. Shake the ingredients and serve over ice. (The Oak Bar at Copley Place in Boston, Massachusetts, has been known to serve the sidecar accompanied by a side glass of ice.)

Feel free to have as many of these as you like provided someone is motoring you home in a sidecar.

# PART 2

# CELEBRATION, INTOXICATION, REGURGITATION

## CHAPTER 5

# Drink Today, for Tomorrow We Die

Life is short—too short to worry about hangovers, some say. On the other hand, life can be very long—too long to not find solace and comfort in a drink, once in a while. For many, "seize the day" translates to "seize the drink," a slap of the hand on the bar, and a hearty call for the bartender's ministrations. Wine and whiskey have waited a long time to be drink-ready, and bottles were made to be opened!

"What do you have to do to get a drink around here?"

—DRUNK, *EARTHQUAKE*

"Who do you have to kill to get a drink around here?"

—NINA, *JUST SHOOT ME!*

"Hey, who do I have to shoot to get a fucking drink around here?"

—OOQ-MI-FAY TAQNUFMINI, *WAR, INC.*

"What do I have to do to get a drink in this place, fart the French national anthem?"

—NEIL SCHWARY, *ONCE UPON A CRIME . . .*

"Who's a girl gotta suck around here to get a drink?"

—BRIDGET GREGORY, *THE LAST SEDUCTION*

"Who do you have to fuck to get a drink around here?"

—EMORY, *THE BOYS IN THE BAND*

"Let's drink until our hearts stop."

—SPACE GHOST, *SPACE GHOST COAST TO COAST*

# "Come on. Let's go drink till we can't feel feelings anymore."

—PETER GRIFFIN, *FAMILY GUY*

"If on my theme I rightly think,
    There are five reasons why men drink,
    Good wine, a friend, because I'm dry,
    Or lest I should be by and by,
    Or any other reason why."

—JOHN SIRMOND

"I only take a drink on two occasions: when I'm thirsty and when I'm not."

—BRENDAN BEHAN

"Fill it up. I take as large draughts of liquor as I did of love. I hate a flincher in either."

—JOHN GAY

"I need a drink, a man, or a massage . . . or a drunken massage from a man."

—DR. CRISTINA YANG,
GREY'S ANATOMY

"My rule of life prescribed as an absolutely sacred rite smoking cigars and also the drinking of alcohol before, after and if need be during all meals and in the intervals between them."

—WINSTON CHURCHILL

"Stay busy, get plenty of exercise, and don't drink too much. Then again, don't drink too little."

—HERMAN "JACKRABBIT"
SMITH-JOHANNSEN

"Trumpets are a bit more adventurous; they're drunk! Trumpeters are generally drunk. It wets their whistle."

—PAUL MCCARTNEY

McCartney's first musical instrument, in childhood, was the trumpet.

"The first drink with water, the second without water, the third like water."

—SPANISH PROVERB

"There's alcohol in plant and tree.
  It must be Nature's plan
  That there should be in fair degree
  Some alcohol in Man."

—A. P. HERBERT

"I've stopped drinking, but only while I'm asleep."

—GEORGE BEST

"There can't be good living where there is not good drinking."

—BENJAMIN FRANKLIN

"The first draught serveth for health, the second for pleasure, the third for shame, the fourth for madness."

—SIR WALTER RALEIGH

"Drink the first. Sip the second slowly. Skip the third."
—KNUTE ROCKNE

"My grandmother is over eighty and still doesn't need glasses. Drinks right out of the bottle."
—HENNY YOUNGMAN

"The trouble with jogging is that the ice falls out of your glass."
—MARTIN MULL

"When I read about the evils of drinking, I gave up reading."
—HENNY YOUNGMAN

"Alcohol removes inhibitions, like that scared little mouse who got drunk and shook his whiskers and shouted: 'Now bring on that damn cat!'"
—ELEANOR EARLY

"It takes only one drink to get me drunk. The trouble is, I can't remember if it's the thirteenth or the fourteenth."
—GEORGE BURNS

"Drink! For you know not whence you came nor why: drink! for you know not why you go, nor where."
—OMAR KHAYYAM

"I am not a heavy drinker. I can sometimes go for hours without touching a drop."
—NOEL COWARD

"Only Irish Coffee provides in a single glass all four essential food groups: alcohol, caffeine, sugar, and fat."

—ALEX LEVINE

"The first glass is for myself, the second for my friends, the third for good humor, and the fourth for my enemies."

—SIR WILLIAM TEMPLE

"No animal ever invented anything so bad as drunkenness—or so good as drink."

—LORD CHESTERTON

"I drink only to make my friends seem interesting."

—DON MARQUIS

"I drink therefore I am."

—W. C. FIELDS

"The decline of the aperitif may well be one of the most depressing phenomena of our time."

—LUIS BUÑUEL

"There is only one really safe, mild, harmless beverage and you can drink as much of that as you like without running the slightest risk, and what you say when you want it is, '*Garçon! Un Pernod!*'"

—ALEISTER CROWLEY

"There are better things in life than alcohol, but alcohol makes up for not having them."

—TERRY PRATCHETT

"There is nothing wrong with sobriety in moderation."

—JOHN CIARDI

"When money's tight and hard to get
    And your horse is also ran,
    When all you have is a heap of debt,
    A PINT OF PLAIN IS YOUR ONLY MAN."

—Flann O'Brien

"A drink a day keeps the shrink away."

—Edward Abbey

"It's not the drinking to be blamed, but the excess."

—John Selden

"One can drink too much, but one never drinks enough."

—Gotthold Ephraim Lessing

"I'm tired of hearing sin called sickness and alcoholism a disease. It is the only disease I know of that we're spending hundreds of millions of dollars a year to spread."

—Vance Havner

"Drinking when we are not thirsty and making love at all seasons, madam: that is all there is to distinguish us from other animals."

—Pierre Beaumarchais

"I am willing to taste any drink once."

—James Branch Cabell

"Everybody gets too drunk sometimes; and even if everybody didn't, I have gotten too drunk sometimes. I haven't hurt anybody. In Ireland we drink a lot. It's part of our culture. I like drinking. I don't think it's a bad thing."

—Andrea Corr

"Drink to-day, and drown all sorrow; You shall perhaps not do 't to-morrow."

—John Fletcher

"I drink when I have occasion, and sometimes when I have no occasion."

—Miguel de Cervantes

"Time is never wasted when you're wasted all the time."
—CATHERINE ZANDONELLA

"When we drink, we get drunk. When we get drunk, we fall asleep. When we fall asleep, we commit no sin. When we commit no sin, we go to heaven. Sooooo, let's all get drunk and go to heaven!"
—BRIAN O'ROURKE

"Nothing makes the future look so rosy as to contemplate it through a glass of Chambertin."

—NAPOLEON

*Hawkeye*: [*offering Cardozo a drink*] Cardozo, booze?
*Captain Phil Cardozo*: When I left the States, I promised my wife that I wouldn't have a drink or another woman, till I got back to her.
*Hawkeye*: [*impressed*] That's nice.
*Cardozo*: Gimme a blast. Make it a short one, I got a date tonight.
—M*A*S*H

"You don't know how to drink. Your whole generation, you drink for the wrong reasons. My generation, we drink because it's good, because it feels better than unbuttoning your collar, because we deserve it. We drink because it's what men do."
—ROGER STERLING, *MAD MEN*

"Drinking provides a beautiful excuse to pursue the one activity that truly gives me pleasure: hooking up with fat, hairy girls."
—ROSS LEVY

*John Linden*: What's the matter? Don't you drink?

*Mary Henry*: Not really.

*John Linden*: Well, I do. And not only do I drink really, I really drink.

—CARNIVAL OF SOULS

"I distrust a man who says 'when.' If he's got to be careful not to drink too much, it's because he's not to be trusted when he does."

—KASPER GUTMAN,
THE MALTESE FALCON

"Ethan, you want a drink? It's part Gatorade and part booze. Gatorade's got the electrolytes that neutralize any ill effects of the booze."

—JIM JARLEWSKI, JPOD

"Good. Tequila and Klonopin, baby girl. A steady diet of that will keep them thoughts away 'til y'alls more equipped to deal with them."

—TRUE BLOOD

"You see, drinking is a matter of algebraic ratio. How drunk you get is caused by the amount of alcohol you consume in relation to your total body weight. You see my point? It's not that you had too much to drink. You're just too skinny."

—FREDDIE, SPLASH

"Well, about every six months, I figure I owe myself a good drunk. It rinses your insides out, sweetens you breath and tones up your skin."

—JACK BURNS,
LONELY ARE THE BRAVE

"I want a glass. About this big. Mmm, no, maybe about *this* big. And I don't care what you put in it—whiskey, hair tonic, rat poison—but whatever it is, when I finish drinking it, I want to be curled up in a little heap, right *here*."

—MARILYN DAVID,
THE GILDED LILY

"When I was eight years old, I woke up in the middle of the night and found my brother pissing on my typewriter. I decided then and there that there was something wonderful about alcohol."

—DAN, *DIVORCING JACK*

*Blackie Benson (Bud Abbott)*: No, you don't want to drink. Remember, every time you go into a bar-room, the Devil goes in with you.
*Heathcliff (Lou Costello)*: If he does, he buys his own drink.

—KEEP 'EM FLYING

*Mary Evans*: Why do you drink all the time? Can't you cut the heavy swilling?
*Maximillan Carey*: What, and be bored all the time?

—WHAT PRICE HOLLYWOOD?

# "Alaska! Where you can't be too fat or too drunk."

—HOMER SIMPSON,
*THE SIMPSONS MOVIE*

"If we don't let druggies and drunks make movies, everybody'd be standing in line to watch three Amish people milk a goat."

—PETER GORDON, *ACTION*

"I like to drink. Sometimes I like to get drunk. Sometimes I like to pass out. I don't hurt anybody with it and I don't drink on the job, contrary to my lieutenant's beliefs. It hasn't killed me . . . at least not yet."

—MICKEY, *AFTER ALICE*

*Connie Wallace*: You know, no matter how fast you drink it the distilleries can still stay way ahead of you.
*Al Wallace*: Yup. But by next week I'll have 'em workin' nights to do it!

—*THE GREAT FLAMARION*

*Garrett Breedlove*: You're just going to have to trust me about this one thing. You need a lot of drinks.
*Aurora Greenway*: To break the ice?
*Garrett*: To kill the bug that you have up your ass.

—*TERMS OF ENDEARMENT*

"Booze, women . . . what in this life that doesn't get you in trouble?"

—CHET FRANK, *REDBELT*

"I always feel sorry for people who don't drink, because when they wake up in the morning, that's as good as they're gonna feel all day."

—HOGAN, *UNDER THE YUM YUM TREE*

This quote has been variously attributed to Frank Sinatra, Dean Martin, Sammy Davis Jr., and Anonymous.

"Sleep! The most beautiful experience in life. Except drink."

—CUTHBERT J. TWILLIE (W. C. FIELDS), *MY LITTLE CHICKADEE*

"I was so jazzed about sobering up and starting a new life; I had to stop at a bar to get a drink just to calm down."

—APRIL RHODES, *GLEE*

"In times like this, my father used to take one large glass of vodka before bed. 'To keep the wolf away,' he said. And then he would take three very small drinks of vodka, just in case she had cubs while she was waiting outside."

—SUSAN IVANOVA, *BABYLON 5*

"Are we still unclear? I'm a functioning alcoholic, you know? And the trick is not to get hung up on the alcoholic but celebrate the function part of the sentence."

—NATHAN FORD, *LEVERAGE*

*Bender*: I need plenty of wholesome nutritious alcohol. The chemical energy keeps my fuel cells charged.
 *Fry*: What are the cigars for?
 *Bender*: They make me look cool.

—*FUTURAMA*

"I think I'll have another drop of Cognac just to keep the wind out of my bones on the way home."

—DR. KERSAINT,
*THE HURRICANE*

"Not only is my intelligence not dampened by alcohol, I actually get smarter with each drink. By the time I'm pissed drunk, my IQ reaches genius levels."

—DR. NIGEL TOWNSEND,
*CROSSING JORDAN*

"I got so wasted one night I waited for the stop sign to change, and it did."

—STEVE KRABITZ

*Dr. Charlie*: JJ, they're your family.
 *JJ*: My family is the best reason I can think to drink myself into a coma.

—*BALL IN THE HOUSE*

"One reason I don't drink is that I want to know when I am having a good time."

—NANCY ASTOR

"Well, to begin with, nobody, and I mean nobody, can talk a junkie out of using. You can talk to 'em for years but sooner or later they're gonna get a hold of something. Maybe it's not dope. Maybe it's booze, maybe it's glue, maybe it's gasoline. Maybe it's a gunshot to the head. But something. Something to relieve the pressures of their everyday life, like having to tie their shoes."

—BOB, *DRUGSTORE COWBOY*

"Mother, I'm in A.A. for real. I go every day. It's not a hobby. It's not a place to pick up guys—most of the time. I'm struggling with sobriety. You haven't even *met* sobriety."

—BILLIE FRANK, *RUDE AWAKENING*

*Holly Tyler*: I'll have a Virgin Martini.
*Waiter*: A martini without alcohol would be a glass of olives.
*Holly Tyler*: That's perfect. And a ginger ale.

—*WHAT I LIKE ABOUT YOU*

"You know, Teensy, ever since you quit drinking you've stopped thinking clearly."

—VIVI, *DIVINE SECRETS OF THE YA-YA SISTERHOOD*

*Lennier*: What kind of drink is that?
*Ambassador Vir Cotto*: I'm not sure. The bartender called it a "Shirley Temple."
*Lennier*: Interesting. I've studied many earth religions and I don't think I've ever heard of that particular temple.
*Ambassador Vir Cotto*: Me neither. But, it's real good.
*Lennier*: Well then. I shall make a point to visit it on my next trip to earth.

—*BABYLON 5*

*Doctor Westford*: If an alcoholic wants me to cure him, you know what I say?
*Zach*: That's a question. That's not a suggestion. OK. What do you say?
*Doctor Westford*: First, stop drinking.
*Zach*: I don't get it.
*Doctor Westford*: Go home and think about it. That's my suggestion.

—*SKIN DEEP*

"You're the one guy that makes me wish they never repealed prohibition."

—JOE, *THE TWILIGHT ZONE*: "A KIND OF STOPWATCH"

*Reggie*: I have been sober for three years.

*Mark*: Yeah right, that's what all the drunks say, how they're gonna get sober and all. They even say they love you but they don't. And then they come home wasted and beat on you and your mother so bad that you gotta hit 'em in the face with a baseball bat!

—*THE CLIENT*

"Thanks for the compliment, but I know how I look. This is the way I look when I'm sober. It's enough to make a person drink, wouldn't you say? You see, the world looks so dirty to me when I'm not drinking. Joe, remember Fisherman's Wharf? The water when you looked too close? That's the way the world looks to me when I'm not drinking."

—KIRSTEN ARNESEN CLAY, *DAYS OF WINE AND ROSES*

"I will not touch the white man's poison—his drugs, his liquor, his swine, his women!"

—MALCOLM X [CHARACTER], *MALCOLM X*

*T. D. Shawnessy*: Flash Perkins, don't you know that your body is the temple of the spirit, and you defile and pollute it with that Devil's brew you have there?

*Orville "Flash" Perkins*: Why, if you say so, pappy . . .

*Shawnessy*: Why don't you come 'round to our next temperance rally. Come 'round and take the Total Abstinence Pledge.

*Perkins*: Why, pappy, I'll take that pledge right now.

*Shawnessy*: Orville, we want men to take that pledge only when they're sober.

*Perkins*: But if they're sober, what's the point in havin' them take the pledge?

—RAINTREE COUNTY

"An American without ice in his drink is unthinkable, if not unconstitutional!"

—ISOBEL VON SCHONENBERG,
HOPSCOTCH

"Let me tell you something I learned in Alcoholics Anonymous. It's a shortened version of the Serenity prayer: 'Kiss my custom-fitted ass.'"

—BILL HILL, TOUCH

*Lenny*: It's a good thing you stopped smoking the magic grass, Homer. You were getting spaced out.

*Carl*: Yeah, we were planning an intervention, but I got alcohol poisoning that night.

—THE SIMPSONS

# "Bring me a virgin banana daiquiri, easy on the virgin."

—MATTHEW, NEWSRADIO

"That is what you do with the drink! You drink it! You can't eat it: nothing to chew! Can't wear it: no straps! Can't smoke it: wet! Drinks are meant to be drunk, much like myself!"

—BILLIE FRANK,
RUDE AWAKENING

"Some things you may want to stay away from while drinking heavily. EBay: not a good idea. EBay and alcoholism, perfect storm of addiction. You'll find yourself up to your ass in George Foreman grills and Sham Wows."

—ROBIN WILLIAMS, *WEAPONS OF SELF-DESTRUCTION*

"Prohibition never stood a chance against exhibition. It's human nature to be free. And no matter how long you try to be good, you can't keep a bad girl down."

—GOSSIP GIRL, *GOSSIP GIRL*

"Love is like an empty bottle of Champagne: you don't refill it, you get a new bottle."

—ANNA, *COME SEPTEMBER*

"Just pour the drink, you fairy fuck."

—PAUL SMECKER, *THE BOONDOCK SAINTS*

"Mary and I used to be like Champagne, fresh and bubbly. But now, we've been uncorked too long. We're lukewarm, flat, collecting flies and there's a cigarette butt floating in us."

—DICK SOLOMON, *3RD ROCK FROM THE SUN*

*Eddie Birdlace*: Where's our fucking drinks?

*Rose*: You boys sure like to swear.

*Eddie*: No, we just like to drink.

—*DOGFIGHT*

*Six*: I think he'd like to think of himself as a man now.

*Chode*: A man? No, being a man takes years of fighting and screwing and drinking and whoring. And fighting a little more and then a lot more drinking and then more whoring if there's time.

—*TRIPPING THE RIFT*

"Men face reality, women don't. That's why men need to drink."

—GEORGE CHRISTOPHER,
BORED TO DEATH

*Violet*: What you need is a drink.
  *Rock Hunter*: And how!
  *Violet*: Maybe two drinks! What'll it be?
  *Rock Hunter*: Something simple. A bottle and a straw.

—WILL SUCCESS SPOIL ROCK HUNTER?

"Choose the one drink you wouldn't give your worst enemy, and give me a double."

—AUTOLYCUS, *XENA: WARRIOR PRINCESS*

"I've known the regent since the first time I came to the Royal Court. He doesn't drink. He cultivated sobriety as his only vice. A break with conventional, accepted behavior."

—LONDO MOLLARI, *BABYLON 5*

"Looks like I picked the wrong week to quit drinking."

—STEVE MCCROSKEY, *AIRPLANE!*

*Dr. Elizabeth Corday*: It's been a long day. I could use a drink. How about you?
  *Dr. Peter Benton*: No. I don't drink.
  *Dr. Corday*: Your body's made up of 60 percent water, Peter. You must drink something.
  *Dr. Benton*: Elizabeth, you know what I mean.
  *Dr. Corday*: Well, have a lemonade, or a Yoo-Hoo, for all I care.

—*ER*

"I never drink intoxicants, Theodorus. I like to experience life in all its agonizing glory. I don't want to dull the sensation for a second."

—CALLISTO, *XENA: WARRIOR PRINCESS*

*Super Hans*: Pint of Guinness, please. No logo on the foam.

*Jeremy Usborne*: No logo on the foam?

*Super Hans*: You don't buy into all that one, do ya? What, the old, "Oo, I've got a clover in me foam, I'm so important." No, what you're doing there is you're drinking an advert, ain't ya, eh, shithead?

—*PEEP SHOW*

## "Look, I don't drink cause I'm sad. I drink because I'm bored and dissatisfied with my life."

—DAVE GOLD,
THE WAR AT HOME

*Chief Inspector Morse*: Isn't it your round?

*Detective Sergeant Lewis*: Do you think another one's a good idea?

*Chief Inspector Morse*: Think? That's why I want it—to think. I don't drink for pleasure!

—INSPECTOR MORSE

"How much money did you give that guy? A wise guy never pays for his drinks."

—LEFTY, *DONNIE BRASCO*

*James Bowie*: I don't deserve mercy. I do deserve a drink. You got anything stronger than water?

*William Travis*: I don't drink, Jim, you know that. I gamble, go to whores, run off on wives . . . but drinking, I draw the line.

*Bowie*: You know, if you live five more years, you might just be a great man.

*Travis*: I think I will probably have to settle for what I am now.

—THE ALAMO

*Vicky*: You know, maybe we shouldn't drink while the kids live here.

*Dave*: Come on, Vicky, we drink *because* the kids live here.

—THE WAR AT HOME

"You'd like a drink better than a poke in the eye with a sharp stub, wouldn't you?"

—Frankie Ballou,
Cat Ballou

*Billy Joe Smith*: What'll you have?
*Philip Marlowe*: What are you drinking?
*Billy Joe Smith*: What I'm drinking is called Aquavit.
*Philip Marlowe*: I'm drinking what you're drinking.
*Billy Joe Smith*: Well God bless you. I like to hear that. People these days go, "Oh, I want a little of this. Oh, and a little of that and a twist of lemon." Balls!
—The Long Goodbye

*Arthur Bannister*: Do you drink?
*Michael O'Hara*: I beg your pardon?
*Bannister*: I asked you if you drink.
*O'Hara*: Whatever's set in front of me. Doesn't have to be wholesome, as long as it's strong.
—The Lady from Shanghai

"Well well well, let's 'ave a drink on it, as me father used to say!
When the truth is nobly spoken, it's respect ye've got to pay!
So fill yer cup an' lift it up and clink, here's how!
No shilly-shallyin', no dilly-dallyin', let's 'ave a drink on it now!
—John Lawless in song,
The Happiest Millionaire

*Sid Jeffers*: I envy people who drink. At least they know what to blame everything on.

*Helen Wright*: If it's so simple, why don't you drink?

*Sid Jeffers*: Me? I have no character.

—*HUMORESQUE*

"I don't drink. You know, the routine grind drives me to drink. Tragedy, I take straight."

—ALEX CUTTER, *CUTTER'S WAY*

# "They can make better booze in a bathtub!"

—JUGHEAD CARSON, *THE WINGS OF EAGLES*

## CHAPTER 6

# CELEBRATIONS
# OF ALCOHOL

Since the dawn of distillation, there have been excellent reasons why alcohol is served at celebratory and memorial gatherings. Consider the funeral wake: family and friends beset by grief need something to lift their spirits. So how about spirits? Hoorah! Raise a glass, share a bottle, and chase the blues away with a chaser. Of course, if mourners drink too much, they may become morose and physically ill, which doesn't help their sorrow.

Consider weddings, reunions, and nights on the town: celebrations are heightened by the dropping of inhibitions and possibly pants. Drink too much, though, and the celebration turns into a wake, in which case you'll need spirits to lift everyone's mood. See? It all comes back to having just one more for the road, or for yourself, or for your new best friend whom you just met.

"At parties like this, Fez, you collect the leftovers of all the unfinished drinks, and combine them to form on giant, über-drink. In this case, a Tom Wallbanger Bloody Sunrise on the Beach."

—STEVEN HYDE,
THAT 70S SHOW

*Gennady*: Lyolik, he doesn't drink. How am I supposed to get him drunk?

*Lyolik*: As our beloved Boss says, when someone else is paying, even the nondrinkers and those with ulcer will drink.

—THE DIAMOND ARM

"Let us drink, gentlemen. Let us drink, till we roll under the table in vomit and oblivion."

—KING HENRY II, BECKET

"Make me a sergeant in charge of the booze!"

—JENSEN, *THEM!*

"Anybody who invites *us* to a party can't be all that bad. And let's not bite the hand that buys the booze."

—TOM REYNOLDS,
*NEVER SO FEW*

"You know, my grandmother always told me to take a nap before dinner in order to conserve my vitality for the serious drinking of the evening."

—EDGAR HOLDEN,
*NO MORE LADIES*

*Ralph Coleman*: Gentlemen, spoils of war!
*Marty Adler*: You're not actually going to drink that, are you?
*Ralph Coleman*: When a man needs a drink, he needs a drink! [*takes a swig*] Burned the hair off my tongue!

—*HUNTER'S BLOOD*

"Booze! I'll drink to that!"

—LANCE KIBBEE [HEARING AN AUDIENCE "BOO"], *THE MONKEES*

*Marcus*: More booze, more bullshit, more butt-fucking.
*Willie*: Sure, the three B's.

—*BAD SANTA*

# "Why is it that the Baptists have all the women and no booze and the Catholics have all the booze and no women?"

—JOHNNY, *ZANDALEE*

## WATERING SPOTS

The next time you are in Boston, forego the usual tourist trap of trying to find the bar where they filmed the 1980s TV sitcom *Cheers*. (It doesn't exist: the show filmed exterior shots at the Bull and Finch Pub, where now cheesy tie-ins and gifts await you.)

Instead, ask your cabbie to take you to 31–37 Stuart Street, the location since 1878 of the **Jacob Wirth Restaurant**. A Prussian immigrant founded this noble eating and drinking establishment, and its current owners honor his memory by maintaining a nineteenth-century ambiance of wood, brass, and polish. Choose from more than one dozen draft beers, try some house wiener schnitzel, and reflect on the wisdom of growing one of those big curly mustaches that you see in the old photos. It's Boston true blue.

"Heat and booze are a bad combination. That's why you never see large, furry animals getting drunk."

—BYRON TOGLER, *ANDY RICHTER CONTROLS THE UNIVERSE*

"The important thing is the rhythm. Always have rhythm in your shaking. Now a Manhattan you shake to fox trot time, a Bronx to two-step time, a dry martini you always shake to waltz time."

—NICK CHARLES, *THE THIN MAN*

"OK, hard drinkers, let's drink hard. I'm buyin'."

—SETH, *FROM DUSK TILL DAWN*

"As we say in Ireland: 'Let's drink until the alcohol in our systems destroys our livers and kills us.'"

—MICKEY, *FAMILY GUY*

"I'm Bender, baby! Please insert liquor!"

—BENDER, *FUTURAMA*

## POTABLE QUOTABLES

Whenever glasses are raised, at least one member of the party is expected to say something benedictory. Now, you could go the cornball route and say something like, "Here's mud in your eye" or "Here's looking up your ol' address," or you could appear cosmopolitan by saying something in a foreign language. Just be sure you get the pronunciation correct and match the toast to the occasion.

- **"Mazel tov" [MAH-zul tov]:** Hebrew for "Congratulations" or, more literally, "Best of luck." Reserve for weddings, anniversaries, and bar/bat mitzvahs.
- **"L'chaim" [luh-HIME]:** Hebrew for "to life." Pronounce as if you were coughing something up a little.
- **"A bon santé" [ah bohn son-TAY]:** French for "To your health."
- **"Salute" [sah-LOO-tay]:** Italian for "A bon santé." To wish good health to a particular person or group, substitute the word "votre" [VOH-truh] for "bon."
- **"Sláinte" [SLON-cha]:** Gaelic for "Salute."
- **"Prost":** German for "Beer!" (And yes, you can say this when drinking wine, too.)

*Dalton*: Sorry, we're closed.

*Ketchum*: Then what are all these people doing here?

*Dalton*: Drinking and having a good time.

*Ketchum*: That's why we're here.

*Dalton*: You're too stupid to have a good time.

—ROAD HOUSE

# "I'm very drunk and I intend on getting still drunker before this evening's over."

—RHETT BUTLER,
GONE WITH THE WIND

*Birdie*: There's a message from the bartender. Does Miss Channing know she ordered domestic gin by mistake?

*Margo Channing*: The only thing I ordered by mistake is the guests. They're domestic, too, and they don't care what they drink as long as it burns!

—ALL ABOUT EVE

"Coughlin's diet: cocktails and dreams."

—BARTENDER DOUG COUGHLIN, COCKTAIL

*D'Artagnan*: Athos, why don't you come join us?

*Athos*: You fight like a man. See if you can drink like one.

*D'Artagnan*: I'll drink anything you put in front of me.

*Athos*: Famous last words . . .

—THE THREE MUSKETEERS

"Oh singin's no sin, and drinkin's no crime, if you have one drink only, just one at a time!"

—KING BRIAN IN SONG, DARBY O'GILL AND THE LITTLE PEOPLE

*Kid Sheleen*: Let's have a drink for old times' sake.

*Butch Cassidy*: Old times' sake? That means you got no cash.

—CAT BALLOU

# "If God had wanted Mexican girls to wear tops, he wouldn't have created tequila."

—ERIC, THAT 70S SHOW

"And that's our task. Liberation. Freedom. Let's toast to Lawrence. Let's toast to our defects. Toast, to our friendship. Drink cold, piss warm."

—HENRY MILLER,
*HENRY & JUNE*

"When I was in college I used to get wicked hammered. My nickname was puke. I would chug a fifth of SoCos, sneak into a frat party, polish off a few people's empties, some brewskies, some Jell-O shots, do some body shots off myself, pass out, wake up the next morning, puke, rally, more SoCo, head to class. Probably would have gotten expelled if I had let it affect my grades, but I aced all my courses. They called me Ace. It was totally awesome. Got straight B's. They called me Buzz."

—ANDY BERNARD, *THE OFFICE*

## WATERING SPOTS

Evidently, some people go to Denver for the skiing or just to spend a long weekend walking around their airport. For our purposes, however, Denver is home to the annual **Great Beer Festival**, sponsored by the Brewers Association. This three-day event welcomes beer lovers the world over to enjoy, indulge, and judge the best that breweries have to offer. In 2010, the Beer Festival fell just shy of 50,000 attendees and over 450 brewers represented. The Festival usually takes place in September or October, and for information on how you can attend, visit Greatamericanbeerfestival.com. And don't drink and ski.

"Ted, these chicks are desperate *and* hot. That's a perfect cocktail: shake well then sleep with!"

—BARNEY STINSON,
*HOW I MET YOUR MOTHER*

"You know, we gotta do it someday. Invite all the jokers from the north and the south for a cocktail party. Last man standing on his feet at the end wins the war!"

—"HAWKEYE" PIERCE, *M*A*S*H*

*Gearshift*: No, Bender, wait. We're the lamest frat on campus. Even Hillel has better parties than us. Please, you've gotta stay and teach us how to be cool.

*Bender*: Hmmm . . . okay, but I'll need ten kegs of beer, a continuous tape of "Louie, Louie," and a regulation two-story panty-raid ladder.

—*FUTURAMA*

"Health: what my friends are always drinking to before they fall down."

—PHYLLIS DILLER

"Look, if it's about that time I puked green slime and masturbated with a crucifix, it was my first keg party, Bobby!"

—CINDY CAMPBELL,
SCARY MOVIE

"I have an aunt who whenever she poured anything for you she would say 'Say when.' My aunt would say 'Say when' and of course, we never did. We don't say 'when' because there's something about the possibility, of more. More tequila, more love, more anything. More is better."

—DR. MEREDITH GREY,
GREY'S ANATOMY

"I'm gonna get me a bottle of tequila and find me one of them Keno girls that can suck the chrome off a trailer hitch and just kinda kick back."

—WENDALL, THE ELECTRIC
HORSEMAN

*Dr. Lawrence Bradford*: What is a cocktail dress?
*Paula Bradford*: Something to spill cocktails on.

—THE EX-MRS. BRADFORD

"As my pappy used to say, 'Stand by your glasses steady, and drink to your comrades eyes. Here's a toast to the dead already, and hurrah for the next to die.'"

—THEODORE "T-BAG" BAGWELL,
PRISON BREAK

*Ben*: To your health.

*Frank Booth*: Ah, shit, let's drink to something else. Let's drink to fucking. Yeah, say, "Here's to your fuck, Frank."

*Ben*: If you like, Frank. Here's to your fuck.

—BLUE VELVET

"Drink to me."

—PABLO PICASSO, DYING WORDS

*Translator*: The general would like to know if you will drink a toast with him.

*Patton*: Thank the general and tell him I have no desire to drink with him or any other Russian son of a bitch.

*Translator*: I can't tell him that!

*Patton*: Tell him, every word.

*Translator*: [*In Russian*] He says he will not drink with you or any Russian son of a bitch.

*Russian General*: [*In Russian*] Tell him he is a son of a bitch, too. Now!

*Translator*: [*Very nervous*] He says he thinks you are a son of a bitch, too.

*Patton*: [*laughing*] All right. All right, tell him I'll drink to that. One son of a bitch to another.

—PATTON

"Ball and chain has gone away, doo-dah, doo-dah! Drink Martinis Naked Day! Oh-dah-di-doo-dah-day!"

—EDWARD MONTGOMERY, *DHARMA & GREG*

"Here's a toast to the roast that good fellowship lends, with the sparkle of beer and wine;

May its sentiment always be deeper, my friends, than the foam at the top of the stein.

Then here's to the heartening wassail, wherever good fellows are found;

Be its master instead of its vassal, and order the glasses around."

—OGDEN NASH

Voice on Tape: "Why don't you come up to my room for a drink? I'll be nude."

The Spore: [trying to learn English] Come up to room for drink, nude be me!

—AQUA TEEN HUNGER FORCE

A wedding is a sacrament . . . a joyous celebration of love and commitment. In Utopia. In the real world, it's an excuse to drink excessively and say things you shouldn't say."

—NICK MERCER,
THE WEDDING DATE

Police Officer: Be careful sir, you shouldn't mix drugs and alcohol.

George Webber: [laughs] You could have fooled me.

—10

"Holy Quervo, baby! Straight white tequila! It's like licking the sweat off of a Tiawana ditch digger!"

—STONE, AVENGING DISCO VAMPIRES

## THE DRINKS CABINET

The modern cocktail party calls for drinks made with infusions and local herbs; the 1990s-theme party calls for super-sweet flavored vodkas and variations on the "-tini"; and the 1980s party calls for concoctions with shocking names and questionable taste.

Behold, then, the slippery nipple:

1 part sambuca

1 part Baileys Irish Cream

1. Sounds simple, but the creation is a little tricky: the sambuca goes first into a shot glass, followed by the Baileys, which must rest unmixed on top. To achieve this effect, slowly pour the Baileys down the tilted side of the glass and straighten, or else pour the Baileys over an upside-down spoon. After the first twelve attempts, you start to get the hang of it. If you can still see straight.

Now, you may be saying, Hmm: anise and sweet creamy tastes— mm-mm! Or not. In case you hadn't noticed, doing shots isn't always about good taste, and the addition to this drink of a cherry (a nipple, get it?) seals the deal.

What can I tell you. It was the 1980s.

*Sara*: What should we toast to?

*Hitch*: Never lie, steal, cheat, or drink. But if you must lie, lie in the arms of the one you love. If you must steal, steal away from bad company. If you must cheat, cheat death. And if you must drink, drink in the moments that take your breath away.

—*HITCH*

*Waiter*: May I take your order?

*Ron Burgundy*: Yes, I am going to have three fingers of Glenlivet with a little bit of pepper, and, uh, some cheese.

*Waiter*: Very good.

*Veronica Corningstone*: Uh, I'll take a Manhattan, and kick the vermouth in the side with a pair of steel-toed boots.

*Waiter*: Certainly.

*Burgundy*: Thank you, Scott. [*To Veronica*] Wow. Quite a drink order.

*Corningstone*: Oh, well, when in Rome.

*Burgundy*: Yes? Please, go on.

*Corningstone*: Uh, do as the Romans do? [*after Burgundy's blank look*] It's an old expression.

*Burgundy*: Oh! I've never heard of it. It's wonderful, though.

—*ANCHORMAN*

*Michael*: [*checking out at a liquor store*] Hey, you're the expert. Is this enough to get twenty people plastered?

*Clerk*: [*seriously considers*] Fifteen bottles of vodka? Yeah, that should do it.

—THE OFFICE

"Alright, listen. I can get you alcohol. I'm going to this party right now, bro. Okay? It's got booze, it's got girls. Booze and girls equals . . . I don't know. Do you? I don't know. Do you? I think you do. Do you?"

—FRANCIS THE DRIVER,
SUPERBAD

"When used separately, women and alcohol can be a lot of fun. But if you mix them, they can turn you into a dumbass."

—RED FOREMAN,
THAT 70S SHOW

"Chartreuse! The only liquor so good they named a color after it!"

—WARREN THE BARTENDER,
DEATH PROOF

"I want to thank you all for coming here tonight and drinking all of my booze."

—BRUCE WAYNE,
BATMAN BEGINS

# "Hey! What kind of party is this? There's no booze and only one hooker."

—BENDER, *FUTURAMA*

*Rudy*: Let's have a bachelor party with chicks and guns and fire trucks and hookers and drugs and booze!

*Gary*: Yeah! Yeah yeah! All the things that make life worth living for!

—BACHELOR PARTY

## THE DRINKS CABINET

If you're one of those drinkers who goes globetrotting instead of bar-hopping, you know that a "shot" means different amounts in different countries. The United States has no standard shot size, except for (don't ask me to explain this one) in Utah, where a shot is 1.5 ounces. Typically, a shot anywhere else in the States is 1 ounce, or 30 milliliters.

In Germany, a shot is 20 milliliters. In Ireland, it's 35.5 milliliters. In Russia, it's 50. At my parents' house at Thanksgiving, it's roughly equivalent to a "Big Gulp" container from 7-Eleven.

Speaking of gulping, not all shots are meant to be downed in one dose, as in America. If you find yourself in Italy, for example, and you're served grappa, the custom is to sip, not to throw it down your throat. (It may have something to do with those Italians wanting to enjoy spirits and not turn their consumption into a contest.)

"Welcome to the club, Number 493. You have become a member of the ancient and noble society of Stonecutters, who since ancient times have always endeavored to shatter the stone of ignorance, to bring forth the light of truth. Now, let's all get drunk and play Ping-Pong!"

—NUMBER ONE, *THE SIMPSONS*

"What are you cut out for? Partying? Chasing tail? Driving drunk? What do you think you are, a Kennedy?"

—GEORGE H. W. BUSH [CHARACTER], *W.*

# "OK, class, today we'll be sitting quietly with the lights off, because teacher has a hangover."

—EDNA KRABAPPEL, *THE SIMPSONS*

*Katy*: Is this really what you're gonna do for the rest of your life?

*Boon*: What do you mean?

*Katy*: I mean hanging around with a bunch of animals getting drunk every weekend.

*Boon*: No! After I graduate, I'm gonna get drunk every night.

—ANIMAL HOUSE

*Telly Peratta*: Do you get drunk every night?

*Ash Correll*: No. Sometimes I'm drunk by noon.

—THE FORGOTTEN

*Gus*: Fuck! How do you just wake up in a room and have no idea where you are?

*Xavier*: I guess you've never been drunk before.

*Gus*: I've been drunk. I spent three years in college.

—SAW II

"Her blood alcohol level was 0.26: blotto. The highest I've ever registered was 0.23, but that was in celebration of my first divorce. I fell down a flight of stairs, didn't feel a thing."

—DR. HAMMERBACK, *CSI: NY*

"Well let me just quote the late great Colonel Sanders, who said, 'I'm too drunk to taste this chicken.'"

—RICKY BOBBY, *TALLADEGA NIGHTS: THE LEGEND OF RICKY BOBBY*

"When you've just emptied two barrels of a shotgun into the head of your favorite bartender, it's a pretty good bet that happy hour's over."

—ASH, *EVIL DEAD: A FISTFUL OF BROOMSTICK* (VIDEO GAME)

"I've lived too long, I'm in the ruck, I've drunk too deeply of the cup, I cannot spend, I cannot fuck, I'm down and out! I'm buggered up!"

—WINSTON CHURCHILL [CHARACTER], *THE GATHERING STORM* (TV MOVIE)

"I'm so drunk, I don't think I could lie down without holding on!"

—TIPSY GIRL, *OCEAN'S ELEVEN* (1960 MOVIE)

## THE DRINKS CABINET

The most effective cure for a hangover is preemptive: that is, don't drink so much in the first place. That said:

- The more alcohol you swill, the more you pee and puke, the resulting effect being dehydration. What you want to drink is not more alcohol (which will dehydrate you further) but water.
- Consider, too, drinking coconut water or coconut juice (not to be confused with coconut milk). Coconut water is an excellent hydrator and its nutrients and minerals reduce acids in the body.
- Fresh air and low to moderate exercise will boost your body's metabolism and thus accelerate the breakdown of toxins. Go for a walk.
- One folk remedy suggests eating honey on toast, for the sugars. You may be better off just eating eggs, as in two scrambled or an egg sandwich. When your body processes alcohol, it produces a toxin called acetaldehyde, whose main function is to make you feel crappy. An ingredient in eggs called cysteine helps break down acetaldehyde. Make that egg on toast using whole-grain bread, which contains vitamin B6—another dose of help for your body.

*Dewey Finn*: [*addressing students*] OK, here's the deal. I have a hangover. Who knows what that means?

*Frankie*: Doesn't that mean you're drunk?

*Dewey*: No. It means I was drunk yesterday.

*Freddy*: It means you're an alcoholic.

*Dewey*: Wrong.

*Freddy*: You wouldn't come to work with a hangover unless you were an alcoholic. Dude, you got a disease!

*Dewey*: Hmmm . . . hmmm. What's your name?

*Freddy*: Freddy Jones.

*Dewey*: OK, Freddy Jones, shut up!

—SCHOOL OF ROCK

"I had a rough night. I had a dream that I drank the world's biggest margarita, and I woke up: there was salt around the toilet bowl. That's not good right there. Thank goodness I didn't eat the worm at the bottom, I'll tell you that right now."

—LARRY THE CABLE GUY, *BLUE COLLAR COMEDY TOUR: THE MOVIE*

"What can I say, Mike? The guy ate like it was his last meal. And the liquor! I mean I've had gunshot wounds hurt less than this hangover."

—SAM AXE, *BURN NOTICE*

"My client feels that it was a combination of liquor and jazz that led to the downfall."

—BILLY FLYNN, *CHICAGO*

*Liz Lemon*: I'm feeling pretty drunk.

*Jack Donaghy*: Well, it's business drunk. It's like rich drunk. Either way, it's legal to drive.

—*30 ROCK*

"So I'm hanging out, and I am just hammered. I wake up in the morning, hung over out of my mind. As soon as I get out of bed, I step into a big pile of dog crap. Keep in mind, I got bare feet on, so folks, I'm cleaning this thing off and I'm noticing corn, I let my dog eat corn you know, chewing gum, looks like he ate a pack of rubber bands. I mean I am ready to scream at this animal, there's dookie everywhere and then I remember, I don't have a dog."

—*Z105 DJ, SATURDAY NIGHT LIVE*

*Ted*: [*in flashback, takes first shot*] Let me tell you something about this brain, OK? [*takes second shot*] Pure alcohol cannot stop this brain. [*takes third shot*] This brain, dear mortals, is no ordinary brain. [*takes fourth shot*] This is a super-brain. [*takes fifth shot*] This brain is unstoppable. This brain . . .

*Older Ted*: And that's all I remember.

—*HOW I MET YOUR MOTHER*

"I don't do penance, I do shots."

—*INDIAN BARTENDER, KEEPING THE FAITH*

# "That was not love: that was excitement, adrenaline, and tequila!"

—*EMILY APPLETON, NATIONAL TREASURE: BOOK OF SECRETS*

Honoring someone—present or absent—by drinking to them is an ancient practice, a way of making a prayerful offering to the gods. In ancient Greece and Rome, when poisoning someone at dinner was the preferred method of assassination (and livening things up before the soup course), the host would get everyone's attention, draw a glass from the decanter to be shared, and drink to everyone else's health: that way, if the host didn't keel over, the guests could relax and only have to worry about there being poison in the soup. Why a "toast"? The commonly accepted belief is that ancient Romans put a piece of burnt toast in their wine to reduce the acidity of the drink.

"I'd like to propose a toast, to my son. He is eighteen today. He has just ordered his first drink. Before he drinks it, I'd like to wish him a long life, a wife as fine as his mother, and a son as fine as he's been. To my son!"

—BULL MEECHUM,
*THE GREAT SANTINI*

"Drinking, crying, cops. Well, it must be Christmas."

—RYAN, *THE O.C.*

"Here's to the drink habit. It's the only one I got that don't get me into trouble."

—COBBY, *THE ASPHALT JUNGLE*

*Elizabeth*: Did you know that the Fentys had an apple farm back in Pennsylvania?

*Ben Rumson*: Apple jack, huh?

*Mr. Fenty*: No, sir, we did not make apple jack!

*Ben*: Then, what did you grow the apples for?

*Fenty*: Mr. Rumson, do you think that everything that comes out of the earth should be used to make liquor?

*Ben*: Whenever possible, yes.

—*PAINT YOUR WAGON*

"[For breakfast] Brasky drank a full glass of liquid LSD with his eggs. Then he slept for eight months straight. When he woke up, he rubbed his eyes and said, "All in all, I prefer gin!""

—*FIRST FRIEND OF BRASKY, SATURDAY NIGHT LIVE*

*Robbie*: Are you drinking, too?

*Julia*: No, it's Coca-Cola.

*Robbie*: Are you sure? There's no rum in that Coca-Cola?

*Julia*: I'm not a big drinker. And if it was, I'd probably be puking more than that kid!

*Robbie*: Oh, I don't think anybody could puke more than that kid. I think I saw a boot come out of him.

—*THE WEDDING SINGER*

"Folks, my firm's done a tremendous amount of marketing research and we've discovered two critical things. One; most Americans feel that Christmas is a time for family. Two; most Americans feel that in order to stand being around their family, for even one or two days, they need to swill as much alcohol as humanly possible."

—*DREW LATHAM, SURVIVING CHRISTMAS*

"When it comes to drinking and driving, my dad is Obi Wan Kenobi. He busted me once for drinking and driving. I woke up, six A.M. Saturday morning, about two months into my senior year. Just hung over, just hammered. I wake up to my father standing over me, wearing a robe, holding a beer. [*mimics opening a beer can*] 'HEY! Why don't you get up and explain to me why the car's parked at such an odd angle . . . on the porch . . . across the street.'"

—*CHRISTOPHER TITUS, NORMAN ROCKWELL IS BLEEDING*

"My father? A hard-drinking man from the '70s. We actually have no pictures of my dad where he is *not* holding a beer: weddings, funerals, water skiing, parent-teacher conference. When I got sick around him as a kid growing up, he'd always warm me up a shot of 100 proof whiskey. Never got sick . . . that I can remember."

—CHRISTOPHER TITUS, *NORMAN ROCKWELL IS BLEEDING* (TV MOVIE)

*Barry McMullen*: [*after someone mentions their father*] Speaking of our favorite wife-beating, child-abusing alcoholic, I went to the cemetery today.

*Patrick*: And?

*Barry*: And I'm happy to report that he's still dead.

—*THE BROTHERS MCMULLEN*

"And now that you have a child, you have to clean up your act, 'cause you can't drink anymore. You can't come home drunk and go, 'Hey, here's a little switch: Daddy's gonna throw up on you!'"

—ROBIN WILLIAMS

*Beth*: It's just like Thanksgiving.

*Jimmy*: Yeah well, it would be if my grandpa were here, all drunk, talking about "those dang homosectionals."

—*ROCK ME, BABY*

"I don't need a birthday, 'cause I buy myself all the presents I need. And because of my drinking, they're often a surprise."

—TRACY JORDAN, *30 ROCK*

*Rita*: What should we drink to?

*Phil*: I'd like to say a prayer and drink to world peace.

—*GROUNDHOG DAY*

"When I first came here, I thought every day was gonna be a Van Halen video: hot chicks wearing bikinis riding around on roller skates drinking cocktails by the pool. Damn you, Van Halen."

—NIKKI, *SPREAD*

*Lois Lane*: Um, um, would you like a glass of wine?

*Superman*: Uh, no, no thanks. I never drink when I fly.

—*SUPERMAN*

*Andie*: So what do you want to drink?

*Duckie*: Oh you know, beer, scotch, juice box. Whatever.

—PRETTY IN PINK

"Ah, come on! It's Christmas Eve! I could be home right now, drinking this monster eggnog my brother makes with lighter fluid."

—CHARLES DE MAR, *BETTER OFF DEAD . . .*

*Marion Kerby*: Let's go have some dinner.

*Cosmo Topper*: Oh no, we cannot eat on an empty stomach!

*Marion Kerby*: Then we better have a few drinks first!

—*TOPPER*

"Ahh, uncomfortable silences and alcohol. Just like Thanks-giving at home."

—J. D., *SCRUBS*

## CHAPTER 7

# "I'M NOT SO THINK AS YOU DRUNK I AM!"

Drinking coffee makes you more awake. Drinking warm milk makes you sleepy. Drinking battery acid makes you my aunt Joan.

Unfortunately, one of the by-products of drinking alcohol is not increased self-awareness: hence the difficulty in letting a drinker know that he has had enough, that she has a drinking problem, or that he should not get behind the wheel of that car, especially if the car is still in the showroom.

When it comes to drunks, we do our best because we would hope for and expect the same from our friends. Sometimes—okay, make that most of the time—things get a little messy, but that doesn't mean they can't get a little funny, too.

*Ben*: Let's talk wine. Karen, you have any preference?

*Karen*: Honey, I'd suck the alcohol out of a deodorant stick, so you're asking the wrong gal.

—WILL & GRACE

# "My daddy . . . he'd walk forty miles for liquor but not forty inches for kindness."

—COLD MOUNTAIN

"My mother loves anything that holds liquor. That's why she married my dad!"

—CAROLINE IN THE CITY

"When the beer companies say 'know when to say when' . . . . You don't ask a drunk to know when to say when! Why don't *you* guys say when to say when? *You're* the experts on beer! You're too drunk to drive when you can't carry a drink with you to the car."

—GALLAGHER,
WE NEED A HERO

## THE DRINKS CABINET

Pop—or soda pop, soda, cola, or Coke, allowing for regional differences—is a decent drink on its own but can be adulterated (that is, made suitable for adults) with a little help from some alcohol. Best of all, these concoctions don't have sissy names.

- **Southern belle** = Southern Comfort and root beer
- **Cuba libre** = Coca-Cola, rum, and lime
- **Cuba light** = Cuba libre using Diet Coke
- **Rum highball** = rum, ginger ale, and lime
- **Jack Sprite** = whiskey (such as Jack Daniels) and Sprite
- **Pimm's Cup** = Pimm's No. 1 Cup and Sprite
- **Seven and Seven** = Seagram's 7 whiskey and 7-Up
- **Lonkero** = gin and Fresca

*Frank Davies*: Look, let me tell you something, I run that bar back there. Every day I see people coming and drinking themselves stupid. You know why?

*Jade Anderson*: I'm not an alcoholic.

*Frank Davies*: I didn't say you were an alcoholic. But you're alone, and that's where it starts. Believe me. I know.

—*EASY KILL*

"I was so drunk, I thought a tube of toothpaste was astronaut food."

—*THE OTHER GUYS*

"Alcoholism is the only disease that you can get yelled at for having."

—MITCH HEDBERG

"The chief reason for drinking is the desire to behave in a certain way, and to be able to blame it on alcohol."

—MIGNON MCLAUGHLIN

"The difference between a drunk and an alcoholic is that a drunk doesn't have to attend all those meetings."

—ARTHUR LEWIS

"I never turned to drink. It seemed to turn to me."

—Brendan Behan

"Cigarettes and coffee: an alcoholic's best friend."

—Gerard Way

"The intermediate stage between socialism and capitalism is alcoholism."

—Norman Brenner

"With such compelling information, the question is why haven't we been able to do more to prevent the crisis of underage drinking? The answer is: the alcohol industry."

—Lucille Roybal-Allard

"I drink too much. The last time I gave a urine sample it had an olive in it."

—Rodney Dangerfield

"Alcohol is a very patient drug. It will wait for the alcoholic to pick it up one more time."

—MERCEDES MCCAMBRIDGE

"I once heard a sober alcoholic say that drinking never made him happy, but it made him feel like he was going to be happy in about fifteen minutes. That was exactly it, and I couldn't understand why the happiness never came, couldn't see the flaw in my thinking, couldn't see that alcohol kept me trapped in a world of illusion, procrastination, paralysis. I lived always in the future, never in the present."

—HEATHER KING

"An alcoholic has been lightly defined as a man who drinks more than his own doctor."

—ALVAN L. BARACH

"A drinker has a hole under his nose that all his money runs into."

—THOMAS FULLER

"Scientists announced that they have located the gene for alcoholism. Scientists say they found it at a party, talking way too loudly."

—CONAN O'BRIEN

"I became a very angry person and it was all due to alcoholism."

—CHRISTOPHER ATKINS

"The contrast which exists between the abstemious man and the drunkard is this: the former governs his affairs, but the affairs of the latter govern him."

—WILLIAM SCOTT DOWNEY

"Alcoholism is the disease of more."

—CAROLINE KNAPP

"Another thing you don't want to do while really drunk is get a tattoo. I did. I got really loaded, I got a tattoo in Mandarin that says 'happiness and laughter' right here. I think it says that. I've never had a Chinese person that close to my balls going, 'That's what it says.'

But I had a friend get really fucked up, and he got a tattoo in Mandarin that's supposed to say 'golden warrior,' and a Chinese friend said, 'No, it says "ass monkey."'

Then the idiot went out and got drunk again, and got a tattoo in Hindu that was supposed to say 'dawn of enlightenment.' And a Hindu friend said, 'No, it says "deliveries on Tuesday."'

So he is now the ass monkey who delivers on Tuesday for the rest of his life."

—ROBIN WILLIAMS, *WEAPONS OF SELF-DESTRUCTION*

"Under the pressure of the cares and sorrows of our mortal condition, men have at all times, and in all countries, called in some physical aid to their moral consolations—wine, beer, opium, brandy, or tobacco."

—EDMUND BURKE

"He tried a 12-step program but he got so drunk he fell down the steps!"

—AGNES MENURE, *RELATIVE STRANGERS*

"Alcoholism isn't a spectator sport. Eventually the whole family gets to play."

—JOYCE REBETA-BURDITT

"Killing someone whether you intend to or not is an antisocial act, drinking is antisocial behavior (even if you are only a so-called 'social drinker'), so killing people with your car because you are drunk is very antisocial."

—CHARITY HAGGETT

"Two drinks a day, on or off stage. Two drinks a day. Two drinks a day! TWO drinks a day! It doesn't work! Not when you want eleven. And not when you start shopping for wineglasses in the vase department at Bloomingdale's."

—ELAINE STRITCH, *AT LIBERTY*

*Mrs. Flynn*: You read like an actor . . . and you drink like one. Would you take advice from the likes of me?

*Dupin*: Ma'am, I take advice as easily as I take a drink. The only trouble with me is I've never been able to make good use of either.

—*THE MAN WITH A CLOAK*

"My father was an alcoholic. Mean fuckin' drunk. Used to come home hammered, looking to whale on someone. So I had to provoke him, so he wouldn't go after my mother and little brother. Interesting nights were when he wore his rings."

—WILL, *GOOD WILL HUNTING*

"I just got back from Scotland. People fucking drink there! Oh my God! There's more vomit in the street than dog shit."

—MARGARET CHO, *NOTORIOUS C.H.O.*

# "Why did I get drunk? I do stupid things when I'm drunk . . . like sleep with my husband!"

—Jenna, Waitress

*Leo McGarry*: You have an interesting conversational style, do you know that?

*Ainsley Hayes*: It's a nervous condition.

*Leo*: I used to have a nervous condition.

*Ainsley*: How did yours manifest itself?

*Leo*: I drank a lot of scotch.

*Ainsley*: I get sick when I drink too much.

*Leo*: I get drunk when I drink too much.

—The West Wing

*Estelle Novick*: I find most people drink to escape from something. What do you drink to escape from, Mr. Poole?

*August Poole*: The ravages of alcohol!

—The Tunnel of Love

*Bart*: [*watching Jim down a bottle of whiskey in one guzzle*] A man drink like that and he don't eat, he is going to die!

*Jim*: [*eagerly*] When?

—Blazing Saddles

## POTABLE QUOTABLES

The national anthem of the United States began as a poem penned by Francis Scott Key (more a lawyer, really, than a poet) after he witnessed the British attack on Fort McHenry in the War of 1812. Key showed the poem to his brother-in-law, a judge, who liked what he read—so much so that he did two things: he had copies of it printed up and distributed, and, most importantly, he realized that the poem fit the tune of a popular song of the time. Putting the lyrics and tune together encouraged people to sing it, and about, oh, 120 years later, President Herbert Hoover declared "The Star-Spangled Banner" our national anthem. By that time, most everyone had forgotten that the tune to which Key's poem had been put was "To Anacreon in Heaven," a satirical drinking song composed, wouldn't you know it, by a British guy named John Stafford Smith. Yes, my fellow Americans, the next time you sing our national anthem at a baseball game, celebrate the song's heritage by taking a long pull of your cold beer.

# "I'm not a drinker; I'm a drunk."

—DON BIRNAM, THE LOST WEEKEND

*Victoria*: You're an alcoholic.
  *Adam*: Alcoholics have class. I'm a fucking drunk.

—HOW TO KILL YOUR NEIGHBOR'S DOG

"People go, 'Now, Robin, how do I know if I'm an alcoholic?' Well as one, let me give you some warning signs. Number one, after a night of heavy drinking, you wake up fully clothed going, 'Hey! Somebody shit in my pants!' Number two, you have a couple of cocktails, you find yourself on the freeway going, 'What are these fuckers doing going the wrong way?' Number three, you get drunk, you go out for Indian food, you wake up in Bombay with a camel licking your balls. Ta da! You are an alcoholic! And some people say, "Robin, I'm a *functioning* alcoholic!' Which is . . . like being a paraplegic lap dancer. You can do it, just not as well as the others, really."

—ROBIN WILLIAMS, WEAPONS OF SELF-DESTRUCTION

"I'm an alcoholic, I don't have one drink. I don't understand people who have one drink. I don't understand people who leave a half a glass of wine on the table. I don't understand people who say they've had enough. How can you have enough of feeling like this? How can you not want to feel like this longer? My brain works differently."

—LEO MCGARRY, THE WEST WING

"I think I would enjoy being an alcoholic! Very much so. A drinker and a libertine. Never in a relationship, but always in love. At church, they'd call me a whore. But I would fancy myself a spirited individual of grand appetites featuring roast duck, red wine, and well-shaped men."

—CARA-ETHYL, *PIZZA*

*B. J. Hunnicut*: By the way, it's not July fourth. It's like, August tenth.

*Dorsett*: Whaddya know? I've been plastered for five weeks! That's a new record!

*"Hawkeye" Pierce*: In Honolulu, maybe, but not here.

—*M\*A\*S\*H*

*Karen Vick*: You know, when I used to work vice, my partner was an alcoholic, and one night I went over to his house, handcuffed him to a radiator, and made him dry out. And when he finally sobered up, I gave him a choice: go into the department rehab program or chew your hand off for freedom. He chose the program.

*Juliet O'Hara*: Is that a real story?

*Karen*: Maybe it is, maybe I saw it on an old *Police Woman* rerun.

—*PSYCH*

## THE DRINKS CABINET

The movie *Harry Potter and the Half-Blood Prince* gave audiences their first look at "butterbeer"—as well as its effects. After a few draughts, Hermione Granger seemed a little . . . well, more friendly with Harry and Ron, throwing her arms around her chums and faltering a little in her stride. Indeed, at Universal Studios' Wizarding World theme park, the butterbeer they serve is a rollicking hit. But since they won't 'fess up to the recipe, kids and their parents have had to experiment on their own. There are several recipes online, but this by far is the simplest:

1 can cream soda

1 tablespoon butterscotch syrup

The sweetness surely appeals to young mouths, but in the movies, Butterbeer drinkers get a foamy mustache. An easy solution is to foam milk and give the glass a dollop.

*Trixie*: So what are your thoughts of rehab?

*Hank Moody*: Rehab is for quitters.

—*CALIFORNICATION*

*Sandy*: Nobody needs to know. We can say you're taking a trip.

*Kristen*: In this town, a trip is *always* rehab.

—THE O.C.

"It was explained to me in *rehab*, the difference between an alcoholic and a junkie was this: An alcoholic will steal your purse, to buy alcohol, and then be consumed with guilt and remorse and drink themselves to death over it. A junkie will steal your purse, and then help ya look for it."

—CRAIG FERGUSON, *A WEE BIT O' REVOLUTION*

"'He was a convivial fellow'—meaning, he was an alcoholic."

—DAN, *CLOSER*

"All right, remember: alcohol equals puke equals smelly mess equals nobody likes you!"

—ROBBIE, *THE WEDDING SINGER*

This guy knows what I'm talking about."

—CHARLIE KELLY, *IT'S ALWAYS SUNNY IN PHILADELPHIA*

*Charlie Harper*: Sure you don't want a drink?

*Alan Harper*: Drinking alcohol just makes me depressed.

*Charlie*: See, the trick is to drink past that. It's not a sprint, it's a marathon.

—TWO AND A HALF MEN

"Ladies and gentlemen, what you are seeing is a total disregard for the things St. Patrick's Day stands for. All this drinking, violence, destruction of property! Are these the things we think of when we think of the Irish?!?"

—KENT BROCKMAN, *THE SIMPSONS*

*Cherie Currie*: What is this?

*Sandy West*: It ain't baby shampoo. I call it the dirty sink. A little bit of everything from my parent's liquor cabinet. Just a little, so they can't tell I'm dipping into their stash.

*Cherie Currie*: My dad would notice. He likes his booze.

*Sandy West*: Is he an alcoholic?

*Cherie Currie*: No, he just likes it. He says that's the difference. He likes to drink, he doesn't need to drink.

*Sandy West*: I like to drink.

*Joan Jett*: The dirty sink is where we're gonna be puking that shit up tomorrow.

—*The Runaways*

"You don't want to turn into the town drunk, Eddie. Not in Manhattan."

—Dorothy Parker [character], *Mrs. Parker and the Vicious Circle*

*Dwight Conrad*: I heard alcohol makes you stupid.

*Fry*: No I'm . . . doesn't!

—*Futurama*

"Yeah, I'm not an alcoholic actually. Yeah . . . I'm only here because I got a little drunk and I threw a flaming bag of feces into a building and I kind of burnt it down a little bit, you know, but I wasn't trying to burn it down I was trying to make the place smell really bad and get rid of this guy. *Phil Leotardo*: We're friends of your son, from Alcoholics Anonymous.

*Joanne Moltisanti*: What's your name?

*Phil Leotardo*: We're anonymous.

—*The Sopranos*

## THE DRINKS CABINET

Should anyone dispute that a swift belt counts for one's recommended daily allowance of fruit, vegetables, or grains, please note the primary source of the spirits below:

- **vodka** = potatoes
- **rye whiskey** = rye
- **bourbon** = corn
- **malt whiskey** = malted barley
- **American whiskey** = cereal grains
- **gin** = juniper berries
- **scotch** = malted barley
- **brandy** = distilled wine (i.e., grapes)
- **triple sec** = oranges
- **sambuca** = *Pimpinella anisum*, or anise
- **sake** = rice

*Leela*: Bender, a turtle isn't yourself. Why do you care about it?

*Bender*: Because I also care deeply about things that remind me of myself, like poor little Shelly here.

*Hermes*: What could you possibly have in common with that walking soup mix?

*Bender*: For one thing, we both have a tough outer shell but live a rich inner life. And also . . . well, you know.

*Leela*: You're both alcoholic, whore-mongering, chain-smoking gamblers?

*Bender*: No, it's just . . . neither of us can get up when we get knocked on our back.

*Fry*: What? I've seen you get up off your back tons of times.

*Bender*: Those times I was slightly on my side.

—*FUTURAMA*

*Alec*: You're being arrested for drunk driving.

*Billy*: Drunk definitely, I don't know if you could call it "driving."

—*ST. ELMO'S FIRE*

"How is that possible? She's a WASP. Liquor is like oxygen to a WASP."

—DR. CRISTINA YANG, *GREY'S ANATOMY*

## THE DRINKS CABINET

The fuzzy navel is akin to the screwdriver, except that instead of orange juice and vodka, you get orange juice married to peach schnapps. This combination gives the fuzzy navel the ring of teenagers raiding their parents' liquor cabinets in search of a fruity buzz.

1 part fresh orange juice

1 part peach schnapps

1. An optional added ingredient is a shot of vodka, or the substitution of lemonade for orange juice. (Try freshly made lemonade, not that powdered stuff.)

As for the name, the "fuzzy" refers to the peach and the "navel" to the orange. Ain't that clever? Ah, just drink it.

*Harry*: My name is Harry and I am an alcoholic.

*Triple-A Lady*: Sir, this is "AAA."

—*3RD ROCK FROM THE SUN*

"Alcohol increases your capability to drive . . . [*checks the answer*] False? Oh, man!"

—OTTO THE BUS DRIVER, *THE SIMPSONS*

*Leo*: My divorce papers came today. She thinks I'm going to drink.

*Josh*: Sounds like a pretty good reason to.

*Leo*: I'm an alcoholic. I don't need a good reason to.

—THE WEST WING

*Alison Scott*: I was drunk!

*Ben Stone*: Was your vagina drunk?

—KNOCKED UP

*Bev*: What! I'm not an alcoholic! I only had one glass of wine!

*Roseanne*: Well, it doesn't count as one glass if you refill it ten times!

—ROSEANNE

"You might think that getting so drunk that you accidentally marry a women who's six months pregnant is a good reason to stop drinkin'. Personally, I think it's a good reason to keep drinkin'."

—EARL, *MY NAME IS EARL*

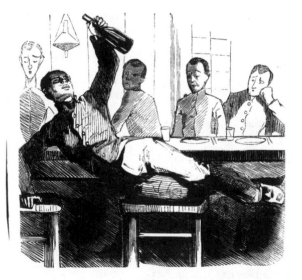

*Roseanne*: Get out.

*Bev*: What?

*Roseanne*: Get out of here before *I* have a drink. You're not just a drunk: you're a carrier.

*Bev*: I'm an alcoholic, Roseanne, don't you know what that means?

*Roseanne*: Yeah, I know what it means, it means you drink like you always drank, only now you say you're an alcoholic because you think that that way you don't have to take any responsibility for anything that you do.

—ROSEANNE

"In my life, a third date turns into a 12-step program."

—JUDY BROOKS,
*ONCE AND AGAIN*

"But seriously, you should've seen my mother. She was wonderful. Blonde, beautiful, intelligent, *alcoholic*. We used to drink milk together after school. Mine was homogenized. Hers was loaded. Once they picked her up for speeding. They clocked her doing 55. All right, but in our garage? And when they tested her, they found out that her *alcohol* had 2 percent blood."

—RUPERT PUPKIN,
*THE KING OF COMEDY*

*Miranda*: What happened?

*Mrs. Doubtfire*: He was quite fond of the drink. It was the drink that killed him.

*Miranda*: He was an alcoholic?

*Mrs. Doubtfire*: No, he was hit by a Guinness truck.

—MRS. DOUBTFIRE

"Well, maybe you should buy an alcohol-powered generator, that way you could urinate into it every morning and have enough electricity for the whole day."

—ELAINE, *TALES FROM THE CRYPT*

"I'm gonna get famous. Then when my career starts to flag, I'm gonna go into a three-month fucking bender, OK? Coke, and fucking pot, and smack, and fucking booze, and drive over people, and beat up my kids, go into therapy, go into rehab, come outta rehab, be on the cover of *People* magazine, and go *Sorry! I fucked up!*"

—DENIS LEARY, *NO CURE FOR CANCER*

"Signor Pal says that drunk, I'm harmless. Sober, I must be pitiful!"

—GIULO THE POSTMASTER, *THE BRIDE WORE RED*

"In my village, the choices were: marry a sober poor man . . . or a drunk poor man. It was a toss-up, really. The sober men would be less likely to beat you . . . but the drunk men would be less likely to keep you pregnant all the time."

—UNIDENTIFIED WOMAN, *XENA: WARRIOR PRINCESS*

"I like the little things. The way a glass feels in your hand—a good glass? Thick, with a heavy base? I love the sound an ice cube makes when you drop it from just the right height. Too high, and it'll chip when you drop it. Chip the ice and it'll melt too fast in the scotch. Good scotch sits in a charcoal barrel for twelve years. Very good scotch gets smoked for twenty-nine years. Johnnie Walker Blue is sixty-year-old scotch!"

—LEO MCGARRY, *THE WEST WING*

"[Alcoholics are] moody little motherfuckers, too. We'll be like, Goddamn it, man. I love you. I'll fucking kill you! But I love you. Come on, step outside. I'll kick my ass!"

—ROBIN WILLIAMS, *WEAPONS OF SELF-DESTRUCTION*

"I had to stop drinking alcohol, because I used to wake up nude in front of my car with my keys in my ass. Not a good thing."

—ROBIN WILLIAMS,
*AN EVENING AT THE MET*

*Marge*: Hello?
*Chief Wiggum*: Uh, Mrs. Simpson, I have some bad news. Your husband was found DOA.
*Marge*: Oh, my God! He's dead?
*Wiggum*: Oh, wait. I mean DWI. Heh, heh. I always get those two mixed up.

—THE SIMPSONS

*Homer*: So they say I might have a problem. [*finishes brushing teeth, rinses with Duff beer*]
*Marge*: [*reading from a pamphlet, "Is Your Spouse a Souse?"*] Homey, do you ever drink alone?
*Homer*: Does the Lord count as a person?
*Marge*: No.
*Homer*: Then yes.

—THE SIMPSONS

"You're the kind of cocktail that comes on like sugar but gives you a kick in the head."

—JIMMY CONNELLY,
*LEATHERHEADS*

*Peter Griffin*: Who's sober enough to drive? [*pause*] OK, who's drunk, but that special kind of drunk, that you're a better driver because you know you're drunk. You know the kinda drunk that you probably shouldn't drive but you do anyway, because . . . come on, you gotta get a car home, right, I mean what do they expect me to do? Take a bus? Is that what they want? For me to take a bus? Well screw that! *You* take a bus!
*Cleveland*: I'm that kind of drunk.

—FAMILY GUY

*Fry*: Bender! You're blind, stinking sober!
*Bender*: That's right! I'm sober and crazy, and I don't know what I might do!
*Fry*: Don't do it!
*Bender*: I don't know what it is yet!

—FUTURAMA

*B. J. Hunnicut*: Hawkeye, the tent is spinning around.
*"Hawkeye" Pierce*: Which way?
*B. J.*: Clockwise.
*"Hawkeye"*: Mine's going counterclockwise. Maybe together we're sober.

—M*A*S*H

"Before this, the most disturbing thing I ever saw was my dad doing tequila shots off the pool boy. Now, I'd gladly use that image as my screensaver."

—CHANDLER, FRIENDS

"Whoever has the most liquor to get the soldiers drunk and send them to be slaughtered . . . he's the winner."

—UNION CAPTAIN, THE GOOD, THE BAD, AND THE UGLY

"If you're born in Kentucky you've got three choices; coal mine, moonshine or move it on down the line."

—LEE DOLLARHIDE, COAL MINER'S DAUGHTER

"You guys make your own wine? I tried to make tequila once, but I didn't know what was in it besides worms. Pretty gross. It still got me drunk though."

—EARL, MY NAME IS EARL

"My friend Sam may have bruised a couple of federal statutes along the way, but nothin' a gift-wrapped bottle of tequila can't smooth over."

—MICHAEL WESTEN, BURN NOTICE

"Twice I took the name of the Lord in vain, once I slept with the brother of my fiancé, and once I bounced a check at the liquor store, but that was really an accident."

—LORETTA CASTORINI, MOONSTRUCK

"I'll admit I may have seen better days, but I'm still not to be had for the price of a cocktail, like a salted peanut."

—MARGO CHANNING,
ALL ABOUT EVE

*John Baggs Jr.*: Would you call yourself a 'Champagne cocktail-sippin', cock-teasin', downtown barroom whore'?
*Maggie Paul*: Second generation!

—CINDERELLA LIBERTY

*Jerry*: Don't you see? He's Jewish for two days and he's already making Jewish jokes.
*Elaine*: Well, everybody gets drunk the first day they turn twenty-one.
*Jerry*: Elaine, booze isn't a religion.
*Elaine*: Tell that to my father.

—SEINFELD

*Tully*: Why don't you stop drinking? Anybody can be a drunk.
*Henry*: Anybody can be a non-drunk. It takes a special talent to be a drunk. It takes endurance. Endurance is more important than truth.

—BARFLY

"That designated driver's pretty hot. I'd like to get her drunk."

—DANIEL DESARIO,
FREAKS & GEEKS

"If you've ever been too drunk to fish . . . you might be a redneck."

—JEFF FOXWORTHY

*Pam Beesly*: Tell 'em what happened last year.

*Jim Halpert*: I had this huge spider in my baseball mitt . . .

*Pam Beesly*: No, no, the guy who hit on me.

*Jim Halpert*: Oh, some drunk guy hit on Pam last year. Said he was "grabbing her for balance."

*Pam Beesly*: [*pointing to her breasts*] Yeah, you don't grab *these* for balance.

*Jim Halpert*: [*considering*] Well . . .

—THE OFFICE

"I mean, look, no matter how you feel about Bush, watching him speak is difficult. It's like watching a drunk man cross an icy street."

—BILL MAHER, *REAL TIME WITH BILL MAHER*

*Derek Sheperd*: I was drunk, vulnerable, and good-looking, and you took advantage.

*Meredith Grey*: I was the one who was drunk, and you are not that good-looking.

—*GREY'S ANATOMY*

"You ought not to leave me alone on days like this. I can't even get drunk. The faster I drink, the faster things happen to sober me up."

—KARLA, *TEXASVILLE*

"I never told you, but you sound a little like Dr. Seuss when you're drunk."

—ANNA CROWE, *THE SIXTH SENSE*

"Listen. As much as I'd love to stay here sweatin' with the oldies, I'm getting a little woozy from the booze-y seeping from your enlarged pores."

—CANDY PRUITT, *WILL & GRACE*

# "You can always find a gift for a dedicated drinker!"

—ROMAN, *TASTY BITS*

"I am sick of fighting! And, I am sick to death of this whole center of the universe, holier than thou, nothing is ever enough. Oh, how I've suffered, nobody understands me. Somebody fix me a drink and hand me a Nembutol, worn-out Scarlett O'Hara . . . thang!"

—SIDA, *DIVINE SECRETS OF THE YA-YA SISTERHOOD*

*Margaret*: You're drunk!

*Henry Blake*: Oh, that's a dirty lie! And I intend to press charges. The minute I'm sober!

—*M\*A\*S\*H*

*Head of Posse*: Ernie Parsons, having been found guilty by a jury of your peers . . .

Ernie Parsons: I didn't see any jury.

*Head of Posse*: Well, they was around. Anyway, what difference does it make. You gunned down Windy Jones and he was one of our most beloved and respected citizens.

*Ernie Parsons*: I heard he was the town drunk.

*Head of Posse*: Well, now that he's dead, he's one of our town's most beloved and respected citizens.

—THE GUN AND THE
PULPIT (TV MOVIE)

"The man is an alcoholic penis with legs."

—MELISSA CAVATELLI, THE
UNKNOWN CYCLIST

"He's a

girl-drink-drunk."

—DEAN WINCHESTER,
SUPERNATURAL

"Flavored vodka is for sissies and pregnant women!"

—JOY, MY NAME IS EARL

"Alcoholics

are mostly

disappointed

men."

—DOC DELANEY, COME BACK,
LITTLE SHEBA

"One drunkard loves another of the name."

—BIRON, LOVE'S LABOR'S LOST,
WILLIAM SHAKESPEARE

*Olivia*: What's a drunken man like, fool?

*Clown*: Like a drowned man, a fool, and a mad man: one draught above heat makes him a fool; the second mads him; and a third drowns him.

—TWELFTH NIGHT, WILLIAM
SHAKESPEARE

"My pop was real big. He did like he pleased. That's why everybody worked on him. The last time I seen my father, he was blind and diseased from drinking. And every time he put the bottle to his mouth, he don't suck out of it, it sucks out of him until he shrunk so wrinkled and yellow even the dogs didn't know him."

—CHIEF BROMDEN, *ONE FLEW OVER THE CUCKOO'S NEST*

*Sideshow Bob*: Homer, how can one man have so many enemies?
*Homer*: I'm a people person . . . who drinks.

—*THE SIMPSONS*

"Mr. Burns was the closest thing I ever had to . . . a friend. But he fired me! And now I spend my days drinking cheap scotch and watching Comedy Central!"

—SMITHERS, *THE SIMPSONS*

"I had a drinking problem back in those days. There are a few things I don't remember, like, ooh, 1974, 1975 . . . "

—SAM MALONE, *CHEERS*

*Walter Harvey*: Let me be blunt. Are you still a fall-down drunk?
*Jimmy Dugan*: Well, that is blunt. No sir, I've, uh, quit drinking.
*Harvey*: You've seen the error of your ways.
*Dugan*: No, I just can't afford it.
*Harvey*: It's funny to you. Your drinking is funny. You're a young man, Jimmy: you still could be playing, if you just would've laid off the booze.

—*A LEAGUE OF THEIR OWN*

# "I don't drink anymore. I don't drink any less, either!"

—ELSIE, *WHILE YOU WERE SLEEPING*

"Who in this [trailer] park, or even in the whole world, doesn't have problems? Who doesn't have a drink too many times once in a while and maybe even winds up passed out in their own driveway, pissing themselves? Who doesn't drink too much sometimes or who doesn't have a puff from time to time? And who doesn't have problems with the people they love? This is our home. This is our community."

—MR. LAHEY,
TRAILER PARK BOYS

*Roland Sharp*: I gave up alcohol about ten years ago.
*Molly McCarthy*: Didn't like yourself when you were drinking, huh?
*Roland Sharp*: Hell, I loved myself when I was drinking. It was the other people that had the problem!

—MAN OF THE HOUSE

*Elise*: I drink because I am a sensitive and highly strung person.
*Brenda*: No, that's why your costars drink.

—THE FIRST WIVES CLUB

## THE DRINKS CABINET

What do mojitos, daiquiris, orange blossoms, juleps, and tequila punches have in common? Besides being things I commonly order in the course of one evening? They—like hundreds of other cocktails—contain something called "simple syrup": a concoction so simple that to mess it up, you would truly need to be drunk off your ass. Ready?

1. Take 1 cup of water and 1 cup of sugar. That's white sugar, and colorless water. If you want to use less or more water and sugar, just keep the ratio 1:1.
2. Put the sugar and water into a pan, and heat until the sugar is dissolved. No need to stir, but don't walk away to check the game: keep your eye on it.
3. When the sugar is dissolved, remove from heat. Let cool, and put in container (a jar, or even one of those deli ketchup dispensers—without the ketchup).
4. Keep in the fridge for no more than a month.

Now, you can also use simple syrup in baking and making non-alcoholic drinks, but for that, you'll need to buy some other book of quotations.

*Sam Leary*: So how come you never gave up on Frank Castle, like everybody else did?

*Jake*: Because I know what it's like to be given up on.

*Sam*: Who gave up on you?

*Jake*: Everyone and myself. You know how most cops like to go out for a drink after work? Well, I kept moving on up . . . to the drink before work, the drink during work, and finally the drink instead of work. It got to be a real problem; nobody wanted to deal with it, least of all me. Before I knew it, I was down to cleaning empty shells off the firing range. Then along came Frank Castle, ex-Marine commando with a shiny new police badge, and a request to learn from the man who wrote the book on busting bad guys: me. He helped me get my act together, and the rest is history.

—THE PUNISHER

"My father would womanize, he would *drink*. He would make outrageous claims, like he invented the question mark. Sometimes he would accuse chestnuts of being lazy. The sort of general malaise that only the genius possess and the insane lament."

—DR. EVIL, *AUSTIN POW-ERS: INTERNATIONAL MAN OF MYSTERY*

*Coach*: What's your most troublesome problem?

*Norm*: Ah, that's tough to say, Coach. Let's see. I'm overweight, unemployed, separated, depressed, starting to drink too much. Guess my biggest problem is I've never been happier.

—CHEERS

# "You know how I feel about my grandmother but I'd sell her for a drink."

—MIKE, *HIGH SOCIETY*

*Diana*: Never mind all that. Let's get to the important stuff. Booze.

*Dietician*: Do you have a drink problem, Miss Trent?

*Diana*: Only when pubs are shut, love.

—*WAITING FOR GOD*

*Greg*: Come on, Mother, do you really think Dad enjoyed sitting on a blanket in the park watching *Othello*?

*Kitty*: He cried.

*Greg*: That's because you ran out of wine.

—*DHARMA & GREG*

*Max Lopez*: But most of my friends have already gotten drunk. I wanna see what it feels like.

*George Lopez*: Let me tell you a tragic story about someone who started drinking at your age. Grandma. The end.

—*THE GEORGE LOPEZ SHOW*

*Ishmael*: You been drinking, Mr. Munson?

*Roy*: I don't puke when I drink. I puke when I don't.

—*KINGPIN*

*Jeff Dunham*: Do you have a drinking problem?

*Bubba J*: Nah, I have it pretty much figured out.

—*JEFF DUNHAM: ARGUING WITH MYSELF*

# "I gotta get a drink. Sobriety's killing me."

—*FRANK PIERCE, BRINGING OUT THE DEAD*

"A Chief Petty Officer shall not drink. However, if he should drink he shall not get drunk. If he should get drunk, he shall not stagger. And if he should stagger, he shall not fall. And if he should fall, he will fall in such a manner as to cover up his rank so that passersby will think he is an officer."

—BILLY SUNDAY,
MEN OF HONOR

*Frank Beardsley*: Helen, the boys have something to say to you.

*Greg Beardsley*: Mrs. North, I apologize for putting all that gin in your drink.

*Helen North*: Ooh, *that's* what did it.

*Rusty Beardsley*: And I apologize for all that vodka.

*Mike Beardsley*: And I apologize for the scotch.

*Helen*: Scotch, vodka, *and . . .*?

*Frank Beardsley*: Helen, you've been the victim of an alcoholic Pearl Harbor. It's amazing you survived at all.

—YOURS, MINE AND OURS

*Mr. Bradford*: How would you describe Mr. Grundy's drinking habits?

*Archie Bunker*: He seldom buys.

—ALL IN THE FAMILY

*Daniel McMann*: I love to drink, Ernie.

*Ernie*: Yeah?

*Daniel*: Yeah, it makes ya feel good. Is that why people drink?

*Ernie*: Some to be happy, some to forget, some to be brave.

*Daniel*: Ya know, I feel really brave, Ernie.

*Ernie*: No, only cowards get brave that way.

—THE OTHER SISTER

# "I get so damned apocalyptic when I drink."

—HANA GREEN,
THE ARRIVAL

*Kitty*: Red, there are five stages of grieving: denial, anger, bargaining, depression, and acceptance.

*Red*: Kitty, I've got two stages: anger and drinking.

—THAT 70S SHOW

*Myriamme Hayam*: Do you drink for pleasure, Monsieur Lautrec?

*Henri*: Is there any other reason?

*Myriamme Hayam*: Many. My father, for instance, because he sought oblivion. Mercifully, he found it, quickly.

*Henri*: Your father was very fortunate.

*Myriamme Hayam*: Then, do you too seek oblivion?

*Henri*: I meant, to have so understanding a daughter.

—MOULIN ROUGE

*Alec Leamas*: [*yawns*]

*Peters*: Tired?

*Alex*: Aren't you?

*Peters*: No, I didn't have any drink with my supper.

*Alex*: I didn't have any supper with my drink.

—THE SPY WHO CAME
IN FROM THE COLD

"I have a drinking problem? Fuck you, Peck, you're a Mormon. Compared to you we *all* have a drinking problem!"

OSBOURNE COX,
BURN AFTER READING

*White*: Uncle Red, don't you think you have a problem with your drinking?

*Red Stovall*: Only when I can't get it.

*White*: I mean, don't you think you might need some help with your drinking?

*Red*: No, I do quite well all by myself.

—HONKYTONK MAN

# "People say that alcohol's a drug. It's not a drug, it's a drink!"

—CHRISTOPHER MORRIS,
BRASS EYE

"Of course he was drunk! The French always drive drunk! Look at Princess Di's driver! Bombed out of his mind! Do you know what the sobriety test is in France? 'Is the driver's liver functioning?'"

—GEORGE FINDLAY,
THE NEWSROOM

*Jeanette*: I have to go to bed soon. I work in the morning.
*Avner*: What kind of work do you do?
*Jeanette*: The kind that drives you to drink.
*Avner*: We must have the same job then.

—MUNICH

"It is not true that drink alters a man's character. It may reveal it more fully."

—NARRATOR, TOM JONES

*Arkady Renko*: A Stinger, please.
*William Kirwell*: That's a whore's drink.
*Arkady Renko*: I am a whore.

—GORKY PARK

"You raise a colt, you teach it to carry a saddle. You raise a man, you teach him to carry a drink!"

—NICK BARKLEY,
THE BIG VALLEY

*Frederick*: I'll just have a drink.
   *Renata*: Right! Drink your-self unconscious. That's the sort of writer's cliché you've never had trouble adjusting to.
                          —*INTERIORS*

"If drinking is interfering with your work, you're probably a heavy drinker. If work is inter-fering with your drinking, you're probably an alcoholic."
                          —ANONYMOUS

"She was a charming middle-aged lady with a face like a bucket of mud. I gave her a drink. She was a gal who'd take a drink, if she had to knock you down to get the bottle."
              —PHILIP MARLOWE,
              *MURDER, MY SWEET*

"We drink to escape the fact we're alcoholics. Existence is the search for relief from our habit, and our habit is the only relief we can find."
         —KATHLEEN CONKLIN, *THE
                          ADDICTION*

*Harvey Forrester*: [*glaring at his unconscious wife*] Lousy stinking drunk.
   *Joe Friday*: Don't knock her, Forrester, she had a reason to drink: she was married to you.
                    —*DRAGNET 1967*

"I take all the drinks I like, any time, any place. I go where I want to with any-body I want. I just happen to be that kind of a girl."

              —HELEN MORRISON,
              *THE BLUE DAHLIA*

*Arresting Officer*: Sir, have you been drinking?

*Ernest Dalby*: Drinking? No no, no. It was poured all over me.

*Arresting Officer*: Sheriff, pour him into the backseat.

—*Spring Break*

"I drink to bring myself down to the level of the common man. But remember: the common man drinks, so I must drink twice as much!"

—K. Roth Binew,
The Living Wake

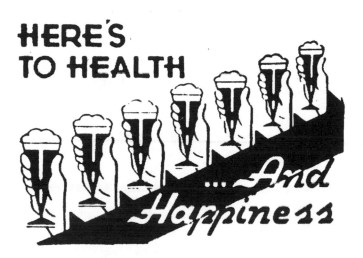

## CHAPTER 8

# HAIR OF THE DOG
# THAT BIT ME

In ancient times, a widely believed piece of bullshit held that if you were bitten by a rabid dog, all you needed to do was rub a bit of the dog's hair on the wound and you'd be fine—or you'd turn into a werewolf, or be consumed by a desire to lick your own balls, something like that. Anyway, that's where we get the phrase "hair of the dog that bit me" and the equally bullshit theory that drinking alcohol helps a hangover. But alas, if strange thinking makes you reach for too much alcohol, too much alcohol leads to strange thinking, as well as to any cure that has even the faintest whiff of working.

Do me a favor? Just read this *chapter very quietly*. I'm going back to bed.

*Lloyd*: What will you be drinking, sir?

*Jack Torrance*: Hair of the dog that bit me!

—THE SHINING

*Sadie*: How'd you get him here? He was out stiff.

*Jack*: A hair of the dog that bit him.

*Sadie*: Hair? He must've swallowed the dog!

—ALL THE KING'S MEN

*Beck McKaye*: Hair of the dog, bro. Want some?

*Quinn McKaye*: Yeah, no thanks. I had a six-pack for breakfast.

—WHISTLER

"I have made an important discovery . . . that alcohol, taken in sufficient quantities, produces all the effects of intoxication."

—OSCAR WILDE

"I feel like I have a hangover, without all the happy memories and mystery bruises."

—ELLEN DEGENERES

# "Grease is the only cure for a hangover."

—CAMERON DIAZ

"I love drugs, but I hate hangovers, and the hatred of the hangover wins by a landslide every time."

—MARGARET CHO

"A real hangover is nothing to try out family remedies on. The only cure for a real hangover is death."

—ROBERT BENCHLEY

"I feel sorry for the '90s, because it was never able to be anything much more than the hangover to the party that was the '80s."

—SIMON LEBON

"Every writer since the beginning of time, just like other people, has been afflicted by what — friend of mine calls 'the fleas of life'— you know, colds, hangovers, bills, sprained ankles, and little nuisances of one sort or another."

—WILLIAM STYRON

"Every time I'd go out drinking I was looking for something new. But it was the same every time: I'd wake up in bed with some person; I had a hangover and a show to do; and the truth is, it was the same every time. But now life is . . . pretty interesting without the alcohol."

—JAMES HETFIELD

"March is the month that God designed to show those who don't drink what a hangover is like."

—GARRISON KEILLOR

"A bad reputation is like a hangover. It takes a while to get rid of, and it makes everything else hurt."

—JAMES E. PRESTON

"Hangovers come with love, yet love's the cure for hangovers."

—RUMI MEVIANA

"You come home, and you party. But after that, you get a hangover. Everything about that is negative."

—MIKE TYSON

"A hangover is the wrath of grapes."

—ANONYMOUS

"Drunkenness is temporary suicide: the happiness that it brings is merely negative, a momentary cessation of unhappiness."

—BERTRAND RUSSELL

"He is a man of thirty-five, but looks fifty. He is bald, has varicose veins and wears spectacles, or would wear them if his only pair were not chronically lost. If things are normal with him, he will be suffering from malnutrition, but if he has recently had a lucky streak, he will be suffering from a hangover."

—GEORGE ORWELL

"Every form of addiction is bad, no matter whether the narcotic be alcohol, morphine, or idealism."

—CARL JUNG

*Peter*: How's it going, Jack? [*Jack takes a drink from his flask*] You know, it's none of my business, but I've learned that the "hair of the dog" saying really doesn't hold much water.

*Jack*: You know, you're right, Pete. It's none of your damn business.

—BOYS OF SUMMERVILLE

"I don't think I've ever drunk Champagne before breakfast before. With breakfast on several occasions, but never before, before."

—PAUL VARJAK, *BREAKFAST AT TIFFANY'S*

"Drinking Champagne in the morning is only for aristocrats. Or degenerates."

—LYOLIK, *THE DIAMOND ARM*

# "Alcohol is a good preservative for everything but brains."

—MARY PETTIBONE POOLE

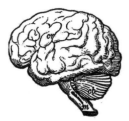

*Ivan*: Why do you take aspirin with Champagne?
 *Alice*: Oh, Champagne gives me a headache.

—*AUTHOR! AUTHOR!*

"Is 'all things in moderation' your motto? Really? Razor-blade to your wrist in moderation? Slam your penis in a car door in moderation? Salad fork plunged into your eye in moderation? I don't follow that old, tired saying. It's too easy to become an alcoholic. Too easy to believe that you need a drink to cope, especially when movies and TV shows like *Bewitched* pounded the 'I need a drink' catchphrase into our brains since childhood."

—DUANE ALAN HAHN

"When I realized that what I had turned out to be was a lousy, two-bit pool hustler and drunk, I wasn't depressed at all. I was glad to have a profession."

—DANNY MCGOORTY

"He that drinks fast, pays slow."

—BENJAMIN FRANKLIN

"I spent a lot of my money on booze, birds, and fast cars—the rest I just squandered."

—GEORGE BEST

# "I ordered you a gimlet. I know you don't drink in the afternoon, but you will eventually, so why not start now?"

—CATHERINE, *THE WOMEN*

"TOPE, v. To tipple, booze, swill, soak, guzzle, lush, bib, or swig. In the individual, toping is regarded with disesteem, but toping nations are in the forefront of civilization and power. When pitted against the hard-drinking Christians the abstemious Mahometans go down like grass before the scythe. In India, 100,000 beef-eating and brandy-and-soda guzzling Britons hold in subjection 250 million vegetarian abstainers of the same Aryan race. With what an easy grace the whiskey-loving American pushed the temperate Spaniard out of his possessions! From the time when the Berserkers ravaged all the coasts of western Europe and lay drunk in every conquered port, it has been the same way: everywhere the nations that drink too much are observed to fight rather well and not too righteously. Wherefore the estimable old ladies who abolished the canteen from the American army may justly boast of having materially augmented the nation's military power."

—AMBROSE BIERCE

"I began drinking alcohol at the age of thirteen and gave it up in my fifty-sixth year; it was like going straight from puberty to a mid-life crisis."

—GEORGE MONTGOMERY

"I don't even drink! I can't stand the taste of alcohol. Every New Year's Eve I try one drink and every time it makes me feel sick. So I don't touch booze. I'm always the designated driver."

—KIM KARDASHIAN

"A good margarita, a good red wine. I like expensive alcohol, but not a lot of it. I don't like to throw up."

—DENISE RICHARDS

"I got sober. I stopped killing myself with alcohol. I began to think, 'Wait a minute—if I can stop doing this, what are the possibilities?' And slowly it dawned on me that it was maybe worth the risk."

—CRAIG FERGUSON

"I had such a wonderful life before drugs and alcohol abuse. I've got that life back now and plan to keep it. Maybe I had to go through what I did to get to this point, to appreciate this life more."

—HARVEY MARTIN

"If you need an excuse for why you don't drink alcohol, you could say that addiction runs in your family and you don't want to try it even once because you may not stop until you are dead in a puddle of your own vomit or smashed into the side of a minivan with children's body parts scattered around your corpse."

—DUANE ALAN HAHN

"I'm glad now, at age sixty-six, that I never used alcohol or tobacco. I've buried a lot of friends who used tobacco or alcohol."

—JERRY FALWELL

"Alcohol is barren. The words a man speaks in the night of drunkenness fade like the darkness itself at the coming of day."

—MARGUERITE DURAS

"One day my wife went and saw the accountant and said she's pulling the plug. She said you guys are done. I said, How bad can it be? Ten grand? She said you're not even close. It came out to almost $50,000 in alcohol for two months."

—ZAKK WYLDE

"That's all drugs and alcohol do, they cut off your emotions in the end."

—RINGO STARR

"The last show we played, I was straight as a die. It did feel weird not to be hiding behind alcohol or dope, but being focused was . . . good."

—RON WOOD

"There is more refreshment and stimulation in a nap, even of the briefest, than in all the alcohol ever distilled."

—OVID

"It's absolutely absurd to even consider voting on Sunday alcohol sales. I am opposed to alcohol period. It doesn't do anybody any good in the long run. It's a dangerous drug."

—JOHN HUNTER

"Teetotalers lack the sympathy and generosity of men that drink."

—W. H. DAVIES

"I try not to drink too much because when I'm drunk, I bite."

—BETTE MIDLER

"I am not drinking now but I cannot guarantee tomorrow."
—KELLY MCGILLIS

"You can't drown yourself in drink. I've tried; you float."
—JOHN BARRYMORE

"Drugs, alcohol, and ego. They are a bad mix."
—DON DOKKEN

"Frankly, alcohol leads to a lot of other things when you start drinking at twelve years old. It is a big problem that needs to be addressed. Frankly, the industry has pushed us back and pushed us back."
—ZACH WAMP

"I think your alcohol intake has to change. You know, usually a big person feels they can drink anything they want to and as much as they want to and I've cut that way back."
—MIKE DITKA

"I once shook hands with Pat Boone and my whole right side sobered up."
—DEAN MARTIN

"I distrust camels, and anyone else who can go for a week without a drink."

—JOE E. LEWIS

"I'm very serious about no alcohol, no drugs. Life is too beautiful."

—JIM CARREY

"I've never had a drink of alcohol or any drug in my life."

—PENN JILLETTE

# "If I go out to dinner with you and you order wine, I leave. I won't be around drugs and alcohol at all."

—PENN JILLETTE

"If they took all the drugs, nicotine, alcohol and caffeine off the market for six days, they'd have to bring out the tanks to control you."

—DICK GREGORY

"If you substitute marijuana for tobacco and alcohol, you'll add eight to twenty-four years to your life."

—JACK HERER

"And I don't really drink a lot of booze. Alcohol will kill you. But I smoke all the pot I can find."

—TOMMY CHONG

"Herb is the healing of a nation, alcohol is the destruction."

—BOB MARLEY

"If we burn ourselves out with drugs and alcohol, we won't have long to go in this business."

—JOHN BELUSHI

John Belushi died of a drug overdose at the age of thirty-three.

"Bacchus hath drowned more men than Neptune."

—Thomas Fuller

"Your body is a temple, but keep the spirits on the outside."

—Anonymous

"I like liquor—its taste and its effects—and that is just the reason why I never drink it."

—Thomas Jackson

"Even though a number of people have tried, no one has yet found a way to drink for a living."

—Jean Kerr

"Drunkenness is nothing but voluntary madness."

—Seneca

*Karen*: Would you like an omelet?
*Nina*: Sure. Put it in a martini glass with gin and no eggs.

—*Just Shoot Me!*

"Miss Morris, I'm perfectly capable of fixing my own breakfast. As a matter of fact, I had a peanut butter sandwich and two whiskey sours."

—RICHARD SHERMAN,
THE SEVEN-YEAR ITCH


"How could you? Haven't you learned anything from that guy that gives those sermons in church? Captain What's-His-Name. We live in a society of laws! Why do you think I took you to see all those *Police Academy* movies? For fun? Well I didn't hear anybody laughing. Did you? Except at that guy who made sound effects. *Vroom. Beep. Honk. Honk.* Heh-heh! Where was I? Oh yeah, stay out of my booze."

—HOMER SIMPSON,
THE SIMPSONS


*John Linden*: [*pours whiskey in his morning coffee*] What do you think, I'm an alcoholic? I just like to start the day off in a good mood.
*Mary Henry*: You must be hilarious by noon.

—CARNIVAL OF SOULS


"If four or five guys tell you that you're drunk, even though you know you haven't had a thing to drink, the least you can do is to lie down a little while."

—JOSEPH SCHENCK


"Whoever takes just plain ginger ale soon gets drowned out of the conversation."

—KIN HUBBARD


"The first thing in the human personality that dissolves in alcohol is dignity."

—ANONYMOUS

*Steve "Fink" Finklestein*: Drunken recall. I gave my subjects massive quantities of alcohol and then I taught them things while they were blacked out. When they woke up the next morning, they couldn't remember anything. But when I got them drunk again, they remembered everything that I taught them the night before. I got it published.
*Landfill*: Where?
*Steve*: In *Maxim* magazine under the title of "E = MC Hammered."

—BEERFEST

*Charlie*: [*slowly making his way down the steps*] Never again! Never, ever, ever again!
*Berta*: You gonna quit drinking?
*Charlie*: Don't be ridiculous! I'm gonna quit waking up.

—TWO AND A HALF MEN

"I never trust a man that doesn't drink."

—JOHN WAYNE

"Everything must be carried out in extreme sobriety."

—GABRIELE NANNI

"My experience through life has convinced me that, while moderation and temperance in all things are commendable and beneficial, abstinence from spirituous liquors is the best safeguard of morals and health."

—ROBERT E. LEE

"I am more afraid of alcohol than of all the bullets of the enemy."

—THOMAS J. JACKSON

"Guys who drink Kahlúa and cream are not power guys!"

—BOATYARD COUPLE,
FAILURE TO LAUNCH

"So you blew me off for a bottle of tequila. Tequila's no good for you. Doesn't call, doesn't write, it's not nearly as much fun to wake up to."

—DR. DEREK SHEPHERD,
GREY'S ANATOMY

"A drunken man is fitly named: he has drunk, till he is drunken: the wine swallows his consciousness, and it sinks therein."

—AUGUSTUS WILLIAM HARE
AND JULIUS CHARLES HARE

"There are hours for rest, and hours for wakefulness; nights for sobriety and nights for drunkenness—if only so that possession of the former allows us to discern the latter when we have it; for sad as it is, no human body can be happily drunk all the time."

—ROMAN PAYNE

"An aching head and trembling limbs, which are the inevitable effects of drinking, disincline the hands from work."

—GEORGE WASHINGTON

"A drunkard is like a whiskey-bottle, all neck and belly and no head."

—AUSTIN O'MALLEY

"He is a drunkard who takes more than three glasses though he be not drunk."

—EPICTETUS

"I have been brought up and trained to have the utmost contempt for people who get drunk."

—WINSTON CHURCHILL

"All excess is ill, but drunkenness is of the worst sort. It spoils health, dismounts the mind, and unmans men. It reveals secrets, is quarrelsome, lascivious, impudent, dangerous and mad. In fine, he that is drunk is not a man: because he is so long void of Reason, that distinguishes a Man from a Beast."

—WILLIAM PENN

"Refrain from drink, which is the source of all evil . . . and the ruin of half the workmen in this country."

—GEORGE WASHINGTON

"First, resolve upon, and daily endeavor to practice, a life of seriousness and strict sobriety."

—DAVID BRAINERD

"You'd be surprised how much fun you can have sober. When you get the hang of it."

—J. P. MILLER

"And must I wholly banish hence these red and golden juices, and pay my vows to Abstinence, that pallidest of Muses?"

—SIR WILLIAM WATSON

"I'm tired of hearing about temperance instead of abstinence, in order to please the cocktail crowd in church congregations."

—VANCE HAVNER

"Prohibition may be a disputed theory, but none can say that it doesn't hold water."

—THOMAS L. MASSON

"This is the way I look when I'm sober. That's enough to make a person drink, wouldn't you say?"

—J. P. MILLER

"Life is good. With sobriety, everything is possible."

—TODD CRANDELL

"Strength of mind rests in sobriety; for this keeps your reason unclouded by passion."

—PYTHAGORAS

"I keep telling people: Don't make me the poster boy for AA because I don't know a lot about sobriety, but I do know a lot about drinking."

—BILLY JOEL

"Laughter is day, and sobriety is night; a smile is the twilight that hovers gently between both, more bewitching than either."

—HENRY WARD BEECHER

"Abstainer: a weak person who yields to the temptation of denying himself a pleasure."

—AMBROSE BIERCE

"It is most absurdly said, in popular language, of any man, that he is disguised in liquor; for, on the contrary, most men are disguised by sobriety."

—THOMAS DE QUINCEY

"The harsh, useful things of the world, from pulling teeth to digging potatoes, are best done by men who are as starkly sober as so many convicts in the death-house, but the lovely and useless things, the charming and exhilarating things, are best done by men with, as the phrase is, a few sheets in the wind."

—H. L. MENCKEN

"The problem with some people is that when they aren't drunk they're sober."

—WILLIAM BUTLER YEATS

"In 1969, I gave up women and alcohol. It was the worst twenty minutes of my life."

—GEORGE JONES

"If you are young and you drink a great deal it will spoil your health, slow your mind, make you fat—in other words, turn you into an adult."

—P. J. O'ROURKE

*Joey Evans*: Good morning!
*Linda English*: What's good about it?
*Joey*: First hangover? Well, there's a first time for everything.
*Linda*: Why do people drink when you feel so awful the morning after?
*Joey*: Maybe because it feels so good the night before.

—*PAL JOEY*

"I'll tell you the secret to avoid hangovers. Don't stop drinking."

—COL. SAUL TIGH,
*BATTLESTAR GALACTICA*

"If the headache would only precede the intoxication, alcoholism would be a virtue."

—SAMUEL BUTLER

"I used to think drinking was the only way to be happy. Now I know there is no way to be happy."

—LAURA KNIGHTLINGER

*Summer Roberts*: [*taking a sip and almost choking*] Uh, and you apparently drink too! What's in this? Lighter fluid?

*Marissa Cooper*: [*takes a sip without blinking*] It's my own drink. I call it a Newport Iced Tea.

*Summer*: It's ten o'clock in the morning. It's a little too early to be drinking.

*Marissa*: For who?

—*THE O.C.*

"If you don't drink, then all of your stories suck and end with, 'And then I got home.'"

—JIM JEFFRIES

*Grace*: Karen, please tell me that you didn't drink your lunch yet.

*Karen*: Honey, I just finished drinking breakfast. You've got to give the liver a little time to digest.

—*WILL & GRACE*

"Habitual intoxication is the epitome of every crime."

—DOUGLAS JERROLD

*Mr. Brown*: I think Mr. Diamond needs a drink. Got any liquor?

*Fante*: How about some paint thinner?

*Mr. Brown*: No, that'll kill him. Anything else?

*Fante*: Hair tonic, 40 percent alcohol.

*Mr. Brown*: Fine.

—*THE BIG COMBO*

"The use of intoxicating drinks as a beverage is as much an infatuation as is the smoking of opium by the Chinese, and the former is quite as destructive to the success of the business man as the latter."

—P. T. BARNUM

"Some of the domestic evils of drunkenness are houses without windows, gardens without fences, fields without tillage, barns without roofs, children without clothing, principles, morals or manners."

—BENJAMIN FRANKLIN

*Macduff*: What three things does drink especially provoke?

*Porter*: Marry, sir, nose-painting, sleep, and urine. Lechery, sir, it provokes, and unprovokes; it provokes the desire, but it takes away the performance: therefore, much drink may be said to be an equivocator with lechery: it makes him, and it mars him; it sets him on, and it takes him off; it persuades him, and disheartens him; makes him stand to, and not stand to; in conclusion, equivocates him in a sleep, and, giving him the lie, leaves him.

—*MACBETH*, WILLIAM SHAKESPEARE

*Michael*: So what's the plan?

*CJ*: The plan is you drink a nice tall glass of Shut The Fuck Up!

—*DAWN OF THE DEAD*

"You know how they say to never drink and drive? Well, never drink and bone."

—BEN STONE, *KNOCKED UP*

# PART 3

# THE WISDOM OF WINE (AND BEER AND LIQUOR)

## CHAPTER 9

# DRINKING MAKES US SMART, FUNNY, AND GREAT LOOKING (AT LEAST WE THINK SO)

Great thing, the frontal lobe (and for you laypeople, I'm referring here to the human brain). This prized area of your cerebrum houses "executive functions," which help you judge the consequences of your actions, determine socially acceptable responses, and retain memories associated with emotion. And guess what, kids: When you drink way too much alcohol—all at once, or over a long period of time—you take a ball-peen hammer to this portion of your brain. Frontal lobe impairment can confuse a person's self-assessment skills: for example, regarding how humorous, suave, or winning we're being. Sound familiar? I hope not.

"You see, every drink of liquor you take kills a thousand brain cells. Now that doesn't much matter 'cause we got billions more. And first the sadness cells die so you smile real big. And then the quiet cells go so you just say everything real loud for no reason at all. That's OK, that's OK, because the stupid cells go next, so everything you say is real smart. And finally, come the memory cells. These are tough sons of bitches to kill."

—RANNULPH JUNUH, THE LEG-
END OF BAGGER VANCE

*Burt*: I don't drink because drinking affects your decision making.
*Arthur*: You may be right. I can't decide.

—ARTHUR

"Never accept a drink from a urologist."

—ERMA BOMBECK

*Lady Astor*: Sir, if you were my husband, I would poison your drink.
*Winston Churchill*: Madam, if you were my wife, I would drink it.

—APOCRYPHAL EXCHANGE

"You can't seriously want to ban alcohol. It tastes great, makes women appear more attractive, and makes a person virtually invulnerable to criticism."

—MAYOR QUIMBY.
THE SIMPSONS

"Alcohol is necessary for a man so that he can have a good opinion of himself, undisturbed by the facts."

—FINLEY PETER DUNNE

"A drunk man's words are a sober man's thoughts."

—STEVE FERGOSI

## WATERING SPOTS

Collecting and buying fine wine can be a very expensive hobby, which is why wine festivals often benefit a charity or worthy cause: any place you can gather people with money is the place to appeal to their good natures. Case in point is renowned **Naples Winter Wine Festival**, which in 2010 marked its tenth year of celebrating good wine, good food, and good causes. (And no need to pack a winter coat: the festival is in Naples, Florida.) Attendees who reveled in the fare of celebrity chefs and world-famous vintners did so knowing they could give to the Naples Children & Education Foundation, which supports the lives of underprivileged and at-risk kids. If Florida is too far for you, go to your local fine wine retailer and ask around: you're sure to locate a smaller and more accessible wine festival in your area.

"Fat, drunk and stupid is no way to go through life, son."

—DEAN WORMER,
ANIMAL HOUSE

*Jordan*: I don't understand how you could have a drink. I don't understand how after everything you worked for—how, on that day of all days, you could be so stupid.

*Leo*: That's because you think it has something to do with smart and stupid. Do you have any idea how many alcoholics are in Mensa? You think it's a lack of will power? That's like thinking somebody with anorexia nervosa has an overdeveloped sense of vanity.

—THE WEST WING

# "Alcohol gives you infinite patience for stupidity."

—SAMMY DAVIS JR.

"The hard part about being a bartender is figuring out who is drunk and who is just stupid."

—RICHARD BRAUNSTEIN

"I know the truth is in between the first and fortieth drink."

—TORI AMOS

"The road to excess leads to the palace of wisdom."

—WILLIAM BLAKE

"Alcohol is a very necessary article. . . . It makes life bearable to millions of people who could not endure their existence if they were quite sober. It enables Parliament to do things at eleven at night that no sane person would do at eleven in the morning."

—GEORGE BERNARD SHAW

"Avoid using cigarettes, alcohol, and drugs as alternatives to being an interesting person."

—MARILYN VOS SAVANT

"Recipe for failure: take one part natural talent, two parts stellar education, mix with easy success and a generous helping of booze, drugs, and women, and immediately set on fire."

—ANTHONY BOURDAIN

"You know when you hear girls say, 'Ah man, I was so shitfaced last night, I shouldn't have fucked that guy?' *We* could be that mistake!"

—SETH, *SUPERBAD*

"The problem with the designated driver program, it's not a desirable job. But if you ever get sucked into doing it, have fun with it. At the end of the night, drop them off at the wrong house."

—JEFF FOXWORTHY

"Then trust me, there's nothing like drinking so pleasant on this side the grave; It keeps the unhappy from thinking, and makes e'en the valiant more brave."

—CHARLES DIBDIN

# "Those that merely talk and never think, that live in the wild anarchy of drink."

—BEN JONSON

"What's drinking? A mere pause from thinking!"

—LORD BYRON

"Drunkenness is the ruin of reason. It is premature old age. It is temporary death."

—ST. BASIL

"Licker talks mighty loud w'en it git loose fum de jug."

—JOEL CHANDLER HARRIS

"After a month's sobriety, my faculties became unbearably acute and I found myself unhealthily clairvoyant, having insights into places I'd as soon not journey to. Unlike some men, I had never drunk for boldness or charm or wit; I had used alcohol for precisely what it was, a depressant to check the mental exhilaration produced by extended sobriety."

—FREDERICK EXLEY

"If we take habitual drunkards as a class, their heads and their hearts will bear an advantageous comparison with those of any other class. There seems ever to have been a proneness in the brilliant and warm-blooded to fall in to this vice. The demon of intemperance ever seems to have delighted in sucking the blood of genius and generosity."

—ABRAHAM LINCOLN

"It is the unbroken testimony of all history that alcoholic liquors have been used by the strongest, wisest, handsomest, and in every way best races of all times."

—GEORGE SAINTSBURY

"You look like a gentleman, but when I've been drinking I'm always wrong."

—LEA, *OPEN ALL NIGHT*

"That's when I realized we might be too drunk to drive, but, we weren't too drunk to pedal. Although I learned a valuable lesson that night: if you're gonna try to fly a bicycle you'd better make sure E.T. is sitting in your basket instead of a twelve-pack of beer."

—EARL, *MY NAME IS EARL*

*Jimmy "The Weasel" Fratianno*: "Sheep-Shaggin' Sean"?

*Sheep-Shaggin' Sean McDoogle*: Why the fuck does everyone call me that? It only happened once. Once! And I was totally wasted. That, and the sheep was totally shitfaced, alright? Alright.

—BEANTOWN

*Pam*: You do realize that we can't serve liquor at the party?

*Michael*: Yeah, I know. Dammit! Stupid Corporate wet blankets. Like booze ever killed anybody!

—THE OFFICE

## THE DRINKS CABINET

Should you try your hand at mixology and experiment with your own concoctions, know that the addition of lime or lime juice traditionally makes a drink a "Rickey."

Traditionally, a Rickey (named after a Colonel Joe Rickey of Missouri) is composed of a base spirit (bourbon or, popularly, gin), a splash of mineral water, and lime. Serve the Rickey in a highball glass.

Technically, then, a mojito is a type of Rickey, given its lime ingredient. Similar "Rickey-like" cocktails include the sour caipiroska (vodka, sugar, lime) and the fruit-flavored Cointreau caipirinha (Cointreau and lime).

Experimenting with Rickies will introduce you to different varieties of limes such as the key lime (tarter than its green cousin, also known for its inclusion in pies) and the Rangpur, or mandarin lime (cross between an orange and lime).

Limes add a strong aroma and tartness to a drink, so if you're buying a drink for a heavily perfumed tart, you know what to order.

*Bluto*: My advice to you is to start drinking heavily.

*Otter*: Better listen to him, Flounder. He's in pre-med.

—ANIMAL HOUSE

"What the hell's wrong with being stupid once in awhile? Does everything you do always have to be sensible? Haven't you ever thrown water balloons off a roof? When you were a little kid didn't you ever sprinkle Ivory flakes on the living room floor 'cause you wanted to make it snow in July? Didn't you ever get really shit-faced and maybe make a complete fool of yourself and still have an excellent time?"

—GIB, *THE SURE THING*

"Being drunk doesn't change who you are, just reveals it."

—THIRTEEN, *HOUSE M.D.*

"Here, have a cock-

tail. It'll help sustain

the illusion."

—MARGARET,
*POOR LITTLE RICH GIRL*

"Poor Bender, you're seeing things. You've been drinking too much, or too little, I forget how it works with you. Anyway, you haven't drunk exactly the right amount."

—PHILIP FRY, *FUTURAMA*

"Her husband was too drunk to know he was too drunk to drive."

—CHARLES, *A BEAUTIFUL MIND*

"It shrinks my liver, doesn't it, Nat? It pickles my kidneys, yeah. But what it does to the mind? It tosses the sandbags overboard so the balloon can soar. Suddenly I'm above the ordinary. I'm competent. I'm walking a tightrope over Niagara Falls. I'm one of the great ones. I'm Michelangelo, molding the beard of Moses. I'm Van Gogh painting pure sunlight. I'm Horowitz, playing the Emperor Concerto. I'm John Barrymore before movies got him by the throat. I'm Jesse James and his two brothers, all three of them. I'm W. Shakespeare. And out there it's not Third Avenue any longer, it's the Nile. Nat, it's the Nile and down it moves the barge of Cleopatra."

—DON BIRNAM,
*THE LOST WEEKEND*

"I don't know if my wife left me because of my drinking or I started drinking 'cause my wife left me."

—BEN SANDERSON,
LEAVING LAS VEGAS

"A proton walks into a bar and orders a drink. When he asks how much, the bartender says, 'For you, no charge.'"

—SHELDON, THE BIG BANG
THEORY

## WATERING SPOTS

Many is the person who has gone barhopping in Chicago only to never be heard from again: that's how many taverns, pubs, and drinkeries there are in the Windy City. If drinking in some of Chicago's history is what you're after, take in **Schaller's Pump** (3714 South Halsted St.). Founded in 1881, it's Chicago's oldest continuously running tavern and is founded on centuries of political, cultural, and athletic history. (The place is within striking distance of both the old and new Comiskey Ball Parks.) The unusual name comes from the legend that its former next-door neighbor, the Ambrosia Brewing Company, used to pump beer into the tavern directly from its casks. If you're Irish, or just want to pretend that you are, indulge in this South Side institution.

"I saw a notice that said 'Drink Canada Dry' and I've just started."

—BRENDAN BEHAN

"Here's another one: drunk walks out of a bar and runs into a guy carrying an antique grandfather clock. The guy drops the clock, breaking into a million pieces. He looks at the drunk and says, 'Why don't you watch where you're going?' The drunk looks at him and says, 'Why don't you carry a wristwatch like everybody else?'"

—UNCLE JESSE, THE DUKES OF
HAZZARD

"My family was a bunch of drunks. When I was six, I came up missing: they put my picture on a bottle of scotch."

—RODNEY DANGERFIELD

"A man walks into a bar with a giraffe. They both get pissed. The giraffe falls over. The man goes to leave and the bartender says, 'Oy. You can't leave that lyin' there.' And the man says, 'No. It's not a lion. It's a giraffe.'"

—MARK, 28 DAYS LATER

*Sydney Bristow*: You know any jokes? 'Cause I could use one.

*Michael Vaughn*: This grasshopper walks into a bar and the bartender says, "Hey, we have a drink named after you." And the grasshopper says—

*Sydney Bristow*: "You have a drink named Doug?"

*Michael Vaughn*: Well, I was going to use "Phil."

*Sydney Bristow*: "Phil" is certainly no funnier than "Doug."

*Michael Vaughn*: Well, I'm sorry. It's a non-humorous joke.

—ALIAS

*Kate*: Hydrogen and Oxygen walk into a bar and see Gold. They say "Au, get outta the bar!"

*Scott*: Um . . .

*Kate*: Because Au is the atomic symbol for gold—

*Scott*: Yeah, I got it.

—JOHN TUCKER MUST DIE

"Say, did you hear about the person of the Polish persuasion who walked into a bar with a big ol' pile of shit in his hands and he says, 'Look what I almost stepped in'?"

—GLEN, RAISING ARIZONA

"A drunk was in front of a judge. The judge says, 'You've been brought here for drinking.' The drunk says, 'OK, let's get started.'"

—HENNY YOUNGMAN

---

"A Frenchman, a German, and an Irishman all walk into a bar. Each of them orders a bottle of whiskey with a fly in each one. The Frenchman says, 'Bonjour, I cannot drink this.' So he gives it back. The German picks out the fly and drinks his whiskey anyway. The Irishman grabs the fly by the throat and says, 'Spit it out! Spit it out!'"

—ROCK MULLANEY,
*CROSSFIRE TRAIL*

"Jo Jo walks into the bar. He's wearin' a solid gold belt buckle this big: says Jo Jo on it. He's got a bracelet on his arm: says Jo Jo on it. He's got a fuckin' necklace: says Jo Jo on it. He's got solid gold cuff links: they all say Jo Jo on 'em. Wait, wait, this little guy walks into the bar and says, 'Excuse me, Mister Jo Jo.' He said, 'Shut the fuck up, I don't want anyone to know I'm here!'"

—JOHN GOTTI
[CHARACTER], *GOTTI*

THE QUOTABLE DRUNKARD

*J. D.*: A three-legged dog walks into the saloon, walks right up to the bartender and says, "I'm looking for the man who shot my paw."
*Ezra*: You might want to work on your repertoire, son.

—<small>THE MAGNIFICENT SEVEN</small>

*Lewis*: What do you call a mushroom that walks into a bar and buys everyone a drink?
*Chris Pratt*: I don't know.
*Lewis*: A fungi.

—<small>THE LOOKOUT</small>

*Nina Van Horn*: Three sailors walk into a bar . . .
*Mr. Henderson*: Hey, I've heard this joke!
*Nina Van Horn*: It's not a joke. I'm trying to tell you about my weekend.

—<small>JUST SHOOT ME!</small>

"So this guy walks into a bar and he says to the bartender, 'Can I use your phone?' The bartender says, 'Sure.' So he wipes his ass on it and the bar—What? Ah, shit. I just told you the punch line. Been telling this joke so fuckin' long, I knew I'd fuck it up."

—<small>OLD MAN, THE AMERICAN ASTRONAUT</small>

"Why did the Irish farmer pour alcohol on his vegetable crop? Because he wanted to have stewed tomatoes."

—<small>ARCHIE BUNKER, ALL IN THE FAMILY</small>

"An American goes into an Irish pub. He said to the bartender, 'Whiskey and ice.' The bartender said, 'There's no ice.' The American said, 'I'll have water.' He said, 'You can't. The water's frozen.'"

—HAL ROACH, *AN AUDIENCE WITH HAL ROACH*

*Bill*: Oh, I remember one time my father came home from a night on the town, which of course had turned into a week, and my mother said, "John, is there anything you won't drink?" and my father shot back, "Poison! I'm saving it for you!" And I and my brother, who's now an alcoholic himself, just about died laughing.

*Lisa*: And this is a happy memory for you?

*Bill*: Of course!

—*NEWSRADIO*

"Excessive intake of alcohol, as we know, kills brain cells. But naturally, it attacks the slowest and weakest brain cells first. In this way, regular consumption of beer eliminates the weaker brain cells, making the brain a faster and more efficient machine. That's why you always feel smarter after a few beers."

—CLIFF CLAVIN, *CHEERS*

*Seth*: [*fantasizing about how he'll get liquor*] You dropped your purse, ma'am. Would you like me to help you with your shopping?

*Old Lady*: That would be lovely! Do you want me to buy you alcohol?

*Seth*: That would be lovely! [*at the cash register, after buying alcohol*] Enjoy your remaining years!

*Old Lady*: I will! Enjoy fucking Jules!

*Seth*: I WILL!

—*SUPERBAD*

*Walter*: It's a big house, we'll divide it up! You stay in your half, I'll stay in mine!

*Anna*: That is such a dumb idea. Sometimes it amazes me you ever passed the bar.

*Walter*: I'm sure it does, you've never passed a bar in your life.

*Anna*: You are so much less attractive when I'm sober.

*Walter*: Thank goodness it's not that often.

—*THE MONEY PIT*

*Harvey Greenfield*: Drink up. It'll make me look better to you.

*Stephanie*: There isn't that much wine in the world.

—*CACTUS FLOWER*

*Jack Withrowe*: Hi. Can I get you a drink?

*Page Connors*: Wow! I've never heard that one before. You really blow me away with your creativity.

*Jack*: Well, I . . .

*Page*: "Well, I, uh . . ." Your recovery's even better! Do you even care at all who I am? I mean, I could be the Antichrist or have the intelligence of a Thermos, but unfortunately those are not the matters the male penis ponders. So please tell me, why did you walk all the way over here to ask to get me a drink?

*Jack*: Well, because . . . I'm the bartender.

—HEARTBREAKERS

*Sgt. Cortez*: You know O'Neil, I like you better when you drink.

*Lt. Jordan O'Neil*: You know Cortez, I like you better when I drink.

—G.I. JANE

*Emily*: Hey, Mags, can I have a beer?

*Jake*: Well, well. So you are gonna have a drink with me.

*Emily*: No, I'm having a drink near you. Entirely different thing.

—THE GUARDIAN

*Jane Avril*: Oh Henri, why couldn't you be tall and handsome?

*Henri*: Two more of these and I shall be.

—MOULIN ROUGE

# "How about you slip into something more comfortable, like a few drinks and some Chinese food."

—CASEY MAYO,
THE BLUE GARDENIA

*Ned*: Can I buy you a drink?

*Matty*: I told you. I've got a husband.

*Ned*: I'll buy him one too.

*Matty*: He's out of town.

*Ned*: My favorite kind. We'll drink to him.

*Matty*: Only comes up on weekends.

*Ned*: I'm liking him better all the time.

—*BODY HEAT*

*Lonnie Bannon*: Probably you think I'm a jerk.

*Hud Bannon*: You don't care what I think.

*Lonnie*: This probably gonna hand you a big laugh, but I do.

*Hud*: You have another little drink and I'll have another little drink. Then maybe we can work up some real family feeling here.

—*HUD*

*Chris Sanchez*: Just because I bought you a drink doesn't mean you're getting laid tonight.

*Street*: So, what does two drinks mean?

—*S.W.A.T.*

You shouldn't drink so much. It melts the lining of your brain."

—DETECTIVE JAMES MCLEOD,
DETECTIVE STORY

*Dennis*: All women are two drinks away from a girl-on-girl adventure.

*Nina*: According to who?

*Dennis*: According to any movie on Cinemax after Dark.

—*JUST SHOOT ME!*

*Ellen*: [*looking at Rodin's* The Thinker] Rodin never said what he was thinking.

*Mickey*: You see, what I think he was thinking was, "Goddamn Rodin. Three drinks and I'm nude."

—*FORGET PARIS*

"*Troy*: You know, I once saw a woman drink one of these, get completely naked, and do The Pony right on this table.

*Annette*: What's your point?

*Troy*: My point is I want to buy you two of them.

—*BACK TO THE BEACH*

"I shouldn't drink, you know. I inevitably say something brilliant."

—JULIAN OSBORNE,
ON THE BEACH

## THE DRINKS CABINET

Any concoction containing an alcoholic element and a nonalcoholic element is a highball, usually served in the glass that bears its name, with ice.

Arguably, the most popular and well-known highball is rum and Coke. Another popular highball is the screwdriver or the Bloody Mary. Some consider multi-ingredient drinks such as the Long Island Iced Tea to be a highball because somewhere in there is cola. But in ordinary mixology, however, one shot of liquor plus ice and the rest nonalcoholic liquid is the standard highball.

Highballs have no standard proportions: i.e., proportions of alcohol to non-alcohol vary from drink to drink, and from bartender to bartender, so depending on your mood, you may want to let your preferences be known ahead of time. That penny-wise bartender may put a drop of rum in your Coke, while your frat brother may pour you a full glass of rum and whisper the word "Coke" over its rim.

*Henry*: Actually I'm not drunk at all, Noreen, and neither are you, because there's no alcohol in these drinks. Sadly, I've used this technique many times. It helps lovely tourists such as yourself loosen up without impairing your ability to stay awake all night and have guilt-free vigorous sex with me.

*Noreen*: Wow!

—28 DATES

*Jake Fischer*: Evening, ma'am. Can I buy you a drink?

*Emily Thomas*: I don't think so.

*Jake*: You don't know what you're missing.

*Emily*: You sure you wanna go with that one? That's, like, your top-of-the-line, A-game material? See, the way I see it, you've got two choices here. Walk away from me, or walk out of here with me and split the cash.

*Jake*: [*bluffing*] Cash? What cash?

*Emily*: The money you bet your friends you could pick me up.

—THE GUARDIAN

*Jane*: You know the real way to tell if a man likes you? Have a drink with him, and if he puts his glass down really close to yours, that means he really likes you and something's definitely going to happen.

*Sally*: You know, I think Patrick does that. I think he does that glass thing.

*Jane*: Of course, as indicators go, an enormous erection's a bit more reliable.

—*Coupling*

*The Devil*: I never drink while I work. Clouds the mind.

*Sam Oliver*: Maybe if you drank you'd be less of a dick.

—*Reaper*

*Morry Machin*: Have you been drinking at all this evening?

*Horace Rumpole*: Of course, I've been drinking at all. You don't think I come out with these blinding flashes of deduction when I'm completely sober, do you?

—*Rumpole of the Bailey*

"Drinking don't bother my memory. If it did I wouldn't drink. I couldn't. You see, I'd forget how good it was, then where'd I be? Start drinkin' water, again."

—Eddie, *To Have and Have Not*

## "I always drink at lunchtime. It helps my imagination."

—Chief Inspector Morse, *Inspector Morse*

## CHAPTER 10

# LITERARY LUSHES
# AND POTTED POETS

Our image of the ink-stained wretch—sorry, "author"—is of a rather forlorn figure in depressed economic circumstances, finding solace and inspiration at the bottom of a bottle. Ernest Hemingway, Jack Kerouac, Raymond Carver: there seems an inevitable and cliché connection between literary greatness and alcoholic worseness, not unlike how we assume until evidence proves the contrary that all politicians are corrupt. But who better to wax eloquent on the raptures and dangers of alcohol than those who wield words with grace and élan?

"When men drink, then they are rich and successful and win lawsuits and are happy and help their friends."

—ARISTOPHANES

"It is impossible to write a compelling novel for men that does not feature moderate to heavy alcohol consumption."

—ESQUIRE MAGAZINE

# "If merely 'feeling good' could decide, drunkenness would be the supremely valid human experience."

—WILLIAM JAMES

"First there was a young guy sitting in front of television in a T-shirt drinking beer with his mother, then there was an older fatter person sitting in front of television in a T-shirt drinking beer with his mother."

—WILLIAM S. BURROUGHS ON JACK KEROUAC

"My third novel, if I ever write another, will I am sure be black as death with gloom. I should like to sit down with—half-dozen chosen companions and drink myself to death but I am sick alike of life, liquor, and literature."

—F. SCOTT FITZGERALD

Fitz's third novel turned out to be *The Great Gatsby.*

"I will never . . . or never have written anything good when I am drinking, or even when the miasma of drink is left."

—EUGENE O'NEILL

"I think a man ought to get drunk at least twice a year just on principle."

—RAYMOND CHANDLER

"Have spent my life straightening out rummies and all my life drinking, but since writing is my true love I never get the two things mixed up."

—Ernest Hemingway

## THE DRINKS CABINET

Root beer isn't only for ice cream floats and belching contests, you know: it can be given a punch—a fruit punch—that'll make a dessert sure to impress your friends.

4 bottles root beer

1 teaspoon allspice

1 teaspoon coriander

2 teaspoons vanilla

3 eggs, separated

4 tablespoons pure maple syrup

1 cup heavy cream

½ cup rum

1. Line a meat loaf pan with parchment paper (with several inches' overlap) and put it in the freezer.
2. Set aside ¼ cup root beer. Add the rest to a medium saucepan. Add the vanilla, allspice, and coriander. Boil on medium-high heat until it's reduced to about 1½ cups.
3. Beat egg yolks in a medium saucepan, gradually whisking in the root beer mixture. Place on low heat and whisk until you have a custard consistency. Place bottom of pan in ice water to chill.
4. In a medium bowl, beat egg whites until softly peaked, then add in hot root beer mixture and continue beating for about three minutes. Add 3 tablespoons maple syrup slowly. Refrigerate.
5. Beat heavy cream until peaked. Beat in remaining syrup. Fold in egg yolk mixture, then fold in egg white mixture. Spread in prepared pan. Overlap paper to cover. Freeze for 6 hours.
6. Heat ¼ cup root beer in saucepan, adding rum and vanilla. Refrigerate.
7. To serve, cut slices of frozen dessert, and spoon rum sauce over it. Yum!

*Cassio*: Is your Englishman so expert in his drinking?

*Iago*: Why, he drinks you, with facility, your Dane dead drunk; he sweats not to overthrow your Almain; he gives your Hollander a vomit, ere the next pottle can be filled.

—*OTHELLO*, WILLIAM SHAKESPEARE

"I usually write at night. I always keep my whiskey within reach."

—WILLIAM FAULKNER

"Drink, and be mad, then; 'tis your country bids! Gloriously drunk, obey th' important call!"

—WILLIAM COWPER

# "Sometimes too much to drink is barely enough."

—MARK TWAIN

"There are two things that will be believed of any man whatsoever, and one of them is that he has taken to drink."

—BOOTH TARKINGTON

"O God, that men should put an enemy in their mouths to steal away their brains! That we should, with joy, pleasure, revel, and applause, transform ourselves into beasts!"

—*OTHELLO*, WILLIAM SHAKESPEARE

"Of all vices, drinking is the most incompatible with greatness."

—SIR WALTER SCOTT

"There are some sluggish men who are improved by drinking, as there are fruits that are not good until they are rotten."

—SAMUEL JOHNSON

"Always do sober what you said you'd do drunk. That'll teach you to keep your mouth shut."

—ERNEST HEMINGWAY

"Alcohol is perfectly consistent in its effects upon man. Drunkenness is merely an exaggeration. A foolish man drunk becomes maudlin; a bloody man, vicious; a coarse man, vulgar."

—WILLA CATHER

"A prohibitionist is the sort of man one couldn't care to drink with, even if he drank."

—H. L. MENCKEN

"Drugs or overeating or alcohol or sex, it was all just another way to find peace. To escape what we know. Our education. Our bite of the apple."

—CHUCK PALAHNIUK

"A man who exposes himself when he is intoxicated, has not the art of getting drunk."

—SAMUEL JOHNSON

"If a man rejoice not in his drinking, he is mad; for in drinking it's possible . . . to fondle breasts, and to caress well tended locks, and there is dancing withal, and oblivion of woe."

—EURIPIDES

"There is nothing which has yet been contrived by man, by which so much happiness is produced as by a good tavern."

—SAMUEL JOHNSON

# "When I drink, I think; and when I think, I drink."

—FRANÇOIS RABELAIS

"Habitual Teetotalers: There should be asylums for such people. But they would probably relapse into teetotalism as soon as they came out."

—SAMUEL BUTLER

"I drink because she nags, she said I nag because he drinks. But if the truth be known to you, He's a lush and she's a shrew."

—OGDEN NASH

"Dost thou think, because thou art virtuous, there shall be no more cakes and ale?"

—SIR TOBY BELCH, *TWELFTH NIGHT*, WILLIAM SHAKESPEARE

"I drink no more than a sponge."

—FRANÇOIS RABELAIS

"The proper behavior all through the holiday season is to be drunk. This drunkenness culminates on New Year's Eve, when you get so drunk you kiss the person you're married to."

—P. J. O'ROURKE

"Water is the only drink for a wise man."

—HENRY DAVID THOREAU

## "Booze takes a lot of time and effort if you're going to do a good job with it."

—RAYMOND CARVER

"I hate to advocate drugs, alcohol, violence, or insanity to anyone, but they've always worked for me."

—HUNTER S. THOMPSON

"Candy is dandy / but liquor is quicker."

—OGDEN NASH

"Alcohol is the anesthesia by which we endure the operation of life."

—GEORGE BERNARD SHAW

"I have taken more good from alcohol than alcohol has taken from me."

—WINSTON CHURCHILL

## THE DRINKS CABINET

British general Sir Bernard Law Montgomery, who led the British Eighth Army in World War II, reportedly liked to have the odds safely in his favor: legend has it that "Monty" didn't like to attack unless he outnumbered the enemy fifteen to one. Inspired by this equation, Hemingway has his character The Colonel in the novel *Across the River and Into the Trees* order "Montgomery Martinis." Shake one up before you head into battle:

3 ounces Gordon's gin

1 teaspoon plus a few drops Noilly Prat vermouth

1 olive

Harry's Bar in Venice, one of Papa's favorite overseas haunts, will make you a Montgomery martini in honor of Hemingway, but their ratio is ten to one. Wimps.

"His was a great sin who first invented consciousness. Let us lose it for a few hours."

—F. SCOTT FITZGERALD

"I have drunk since I was fifteen and few things have given me more pleasure. When you work hard all day with your head and know you must work again the next day what else can change your ideas and make them run on a different plane like whiskey? When you are cold and wet what else can warm you? Before an attack who can say anything that gives you the momentary well being that rum does?"

—ERNEST HEMINGWAY

"The tools I need for my work are paper, tobacco, food, and a little whiskey."

—WILLIAM FAULKNER

"An intelligent man is sometimes forced to be drunk to spend time with his fools."

—ERNEST HEMINGWAY

"My peers, lately, have found companionship through means of intoxication—it makes them sociable. I, however, cannot force myself to use drugs to cheat on my loneliness—it is all that I have—and when the drugs and alcohol dissipate, will be all that my peers have as well."

—FRANZ KAFKA

"Why are you drinking?" demanded the little prince.

"So that I may forget," replied the tippler.

"Forget what?" inquired the little prince, who already was sorry for him.

"Forget that I am ashamed," the tippler confessed, hanging his head.

"Ashamed of what?" insisted the little prince, who wanted to help him.

—ANTOINE DE SAINT-EXUPÉRY, THE LITTLE PRINCE

"My work is the only thing that makes me happy—except to be a little tight—and for those two indulgences I pay a big price in mental and physical hangovers."

—F. SCOTT FITZGERALD

"Ashamed of drinking!" The tippler brought his speech to an end, and shut himself up in an impregnable silence.

—ANTOINE DE SAINT-EXUPÉRY, THE LITTLE PRINCE

"You've got to have all your critical and creative faculties about you when you're working. I never try to write a line when I'm not strictly on the wagon. I don't think anything worth reading was ever written by anyone who was drunk or even half drunk when he wrote it. This is not morality, it's plain psychology."

—EUGENE O'NEILL

"I like to do my principal research in bars, where people are more likely to tell the truth or, at least, lie less convincingly than they do in briefings and books."

—P. J. O'ROURKE

"I have never written a serious word in my life under the influence of alcohol."

—WILLIAM STYRON

"A man's prose style is very responsive—even a glass of sherry shows in a sentence."

—JOHN CHEEVER

"Boozing does not necessarily have to go hand in hand with being a writer, as seems to be the concept in America. I therefore solemnly declare to all young men trying to become writers that they do not actually have to become drunkards first."

—JAMES JONES

"When I have one martini, I feel bigger, wiser, taller. When I have a second, I feel superlative. When I have more, there's no holding me."

—WILLIAM FAULKNER

"I've gone on the wagon, but my body doesn't believe it. It's waiting for that whiskey to get in there . . . to get me going. I never drink while I'm working, but after a few glasses, I get ideas that never would have occurred to me dead sober."

—IRWIN SHAW

"Some American writers who have known each other for years have never met in the daytime or when both were sober."

—JAMES THURBER

"One of the disadvantages of wine is that it makes a man mistake words for thoughts."

—SAMUEL JOHNSON

"Before I start to write, I always treat myself to a nice dry martini. Just one, to give me the courage to get started. After that, I am on my own."

—E. B. WHITE

"I can't write without wine."

—TENNESSEE WILLIAMS

"After a few ounces, the old tunes wake up, the grandeur of jingling anguish, the lick and shimmer of language, the heartbreak at the core of things. . . . At a certain glow-level my brilliancies assured me I was an angel writing in Paradise."

—DONALD NEWLOVE

"Many contemporary writers drink more than they write."

—MAXIM GORKY

"Drinking makes you loquacious, as we all know, and if what you've got for company is a piece of paper, then you're going to talk to it. Just try to enunciate, and try to make sense."

—MADISON SMARTT BELL

"No one, ever, wrote anything as well even after one drink as he would have done without it."

—RING LARDNER

# "I usually need a can of beer to prime me."

—NORMAN MAILER

"I'm Catholic and I can't commit suicide, but I plan to drink myself to death."

—JACK KEROUAC

"Writing is a lonely job, unless you're a drinker, in which case you always have a friend within reach."

—EMILIO ESTEVEZ

"Drinking is an emotional thing. It joggles you out of everyday life, out of everything being the same. It yanks you out of your body and your mind and throws you against the wall. I have the feeling that drinking is a form of suicide where you're allowed to return to life and begin all over the next day. It's like killing yourself, and then you're reborn. I guess I've lived about 10 or 15,000 lives now."

—CHARLES BUKOWSKI

"An alcoholic is someone you don't like who drinks as much as you do."

—DYLAN THOMAS

"We have wasted History like a bunch of drunks shooting dice back in the men's crapper of the local bar."

—CHARLES BUKOWSKI

"Everyone who drinks is not a poet. Maybe some of us drink because we're not poets."

—ARTHUR, *ARTHUR*

"It's always difficult to make conversation with a drunk, and there's no denying it, the sober are at the disadvantage with him."

—W. SOMERSET MAUGHAM

"No poems can please for long or live that are written by water-drinkers."

—HORACE

"Work is the curse of the drinking class."

—OSCAR WILDE

"Art is wine and experience is the brandy we distill from it."

—ROBERTSON DAVIES

"Of the demonstrably wise there are but two: those who commit suicide, and those who keep their reasoning faculties atrophied by drink."

—MARK TWAIN

"A horrid alcoholic explosion scatters all my good intentions like bits of limbs and clothes over the doorsteps and into the saloon bars of the tawdriest pubs."

—DYLAN THOMAS

"No other human being, no woman, no poem or music, book or painting can replace alcohol in its power to give man the illusion of real creation."

—MARGUERITE DURAS

"Frankly, I was horrified by life, at what a man had to do simply in order to eat, sleep, and keep himself clothed. So I stayed in bed and drank. When you drank the world was still out there, but for the moment it didn't have you by the throat."

—CHARLES BUKOWSKI

"For art to exist, for any sort of aesthetic activity or perception to exist, a certain physiological precondition is indispensable: intoxication."

—FRIEDRICH NIETZSCHE

"I am a drinker with writing problems."

—BRENDAN BEHAN

"I was carrying a beautiful alcoholic conflagration around with me. The thing fed on its own heat and flamed the fiercer. There was no time, in all my waking time, that I didn't want a drink. I began to anticipate the completion of my daily thousand words by taking a drink when only five hundred words were written. It was not long until I prefaced the beginning of the thousand words with a drink."

—JACK LONDON

"Teaching has ruined more American novelists than drink."

—GORE VIDAL

**POTABLE QUOTABLES**

In his entertaining memoir *At Random*, book publisher Bennett Cerf relates countless anecdotes about authors with whom he's worked, including James Joyce. To work out the details of publishing *Ulysses*, Cerf went to Paris to meet Joyce and his wife Nora, and he ended up spending several evenings with the couple, including one night when Joyce "got really potted" and insisted, much to his wife's disapproval, on playing Irish ballads at the piano:

"There was a long bench in front of [the piano], and Nora grabbed one end and Joyce the other—both pulling in opposite directions. Suddenly she deliberated let go, and Joyce went staggering back and landed on his behind on the floor against the wall with the piano bench on top of him. Nora said, 'Maybe this will teach you a lesson, you drunken . . .'"

Cerf took that as his cue to leave, but Nora followed him out: "The last thing I heard from [Nora] when I got into the cab was, 'Someday *I'm* going to write a book for you, Bennett, and I'm going to call it 'My Twenty Years with a Genius—So-Called.'"

"So long as I considered myself as the medium of (arena for) my powers, sobriety was out of the question. . . . The even deeper delusion that my art depended on my drinking, or at least was connected with it, could not be attackt [*sic*] directly. Too far down. The cover had to be exploded off."

—JOHN BERRYMAN

"After one drink, it's very hard not to take another, and after three it is even harder not to take three more."

—JAMES AGEE

"[F. Scott Fitzgerald] began to use liquor for posture and gesture, like almost any writer of the 1920s, but by the time he was forty he had found or invented ten or twelve reasons for keeping it up. (Most writers have only four or five.) . . . The most persistent of these was that his creative vitality demanded stimulation if it was to continue to operate. . . . But when Fitzgerald began to drink because he thought he had to, in order to write, he was lost."

—JAMES THURBER

"Bind myself to forswear wine forever I cannot. My vision of the world at its brightest is such that life without the use of its amentities [sic] is impossible. . . . The fact that I have abused liquor is something to be paid for with suffering and death perhaps but not with renunciation. For me it would be as illogical as permanently giving up sex because I caught a disease. . . . I cannot consider one pint of wine at the day's end as anything but one of the rights of man."

—F. SCOTT FITZGERALD

"Of course you're a rummy. But you're no more of a rummy than [James] Joyce is and most good writers are. But Scott, good writers always come back. Always. You are twice as good now as you were at the time you think you were so marvelous."

—ERNEST HEMINGWAY, WRITING TO FITZGERALD

"Drinking made uninteresting people matter less and, late at night, matter not at all."

—LILLIAN HELLMAN

## THE DRINKS CABINET

If you've been reading the Styles section of your major metropolitan newspaper, you've heard that the latest trend among bartenders—sorry, "mixologists"—is fresh ingredients: fresh mint, fresh fruit, fresh herbs. There's no reason why your own home bar cannot follow suit, but don't think that substituting real cherries for the cherries in a jar will be an improvement.

The cherries you buy in the supermarket are likely Bing cherries or black cherries. The cherries in cocktails—maraschino cherries—were originally made from marasca cherries but today are made from Gold, Rainier, or Royal Ann cherries. These cherries are soaked in sulfur dioxide (or alcohol), food coloring, preservatives, flavoring (e.g., almond), and syrup to make them extra sweet. The process also makes them soft and absorbent, so one fished out of your empty glass retains some alcoholic flavor.

Your parents' (or grandparents') drinks usually call for maraschino cherries: Tom Collins, Old Fashioned, and the Manhattan. You yourself may find these cherries as appetizing in your drink as on your glazed ham or fruitcake, which is to say not at all.

If you still want that cherry flavor, try a rum and cherry Coke, or better yet, try maraschino, a clear cherry liqueur.

"A poet without alcohol is not a real poet."

—CONRAD AIKEN

"Drinking makes such fools of people, and people are such fools to begin with, that it's compounding a felony."

—ROBERT BENCHLEY

"When you get drunk there is no difference between you and a lot of drunken advertising men."

—SHERWOOD ANDERSON

"At four o'clock in the morning, when everybody's drunk enough, then extraordinary things can happen."

—JAMES BALDWIN

"You never start out in life with the intention of becoming a bankrupt or an alcoholic."

—RAYMOND CARVER

"I've worn out several kidneys and several bladders already on bootleg rum, but I seem always ready to risk another."

—HART CRANE

"What's the use of winning the Nobel Prize if it doesn't even get you into speakeasies?"

—SINCLAIR LEWIS

"I was always willing to drink when anyone was around. I drank by myself when no one was around."

—JACK LONDON

"I drink exactly as much as I want, and one drink more."

—H. L. MENCKEN

"First, like everyone, I appreciated the effect of slight drunkenness; then very soon I grew to like what lies beyond violent drunkenness; when one has passed that stage: a magnificent and terrible peace, the true taste of the passage of time."

—GUY DEBORD

"I never want to read about another alcoholic; alcoholism is the enemy of art and the curse of Western civilization. It is neither poetic nor amusing. I am not referring to people getting drunk but to the gradual blotting out of the sensibilities and the destruction of personal relationships in the long-drawn social suicide."

—CYRIL CONNOLLY

"Don't drink to get

drunk. Drink to

enjoy life."

—JACK KEROUAC

"I'm ombibulous. I drink every known alcoholic drink and enjoy them all."

—H. L. MENCKEN

CHAPTER 11

# DRINKS GO TO THE MOVIES

Alcohol (and its abuse) makes for conflict, comedy, pathos, bathos, and irony: all key ingredients for a satisfying flick. Moreover, alcoholism is a disease most everyone can relate to, allowing not only for good visuals but also good sound effects (usually behind a closed bathroom door). There have been some poignant and powerful movies about alcoholics, plenty of movies featuring alcoholics, and even more films directed by alcoholics.

"I'm going to be a great film star! That is, if booze and sex don't get me first."

—SALLY, *CABARET*

# "Then how about a night- cap on the company? My company."

—JAMES BOND, *THE SPY WHO LOVED ME*

*Jane*: Would you like a nightcap?
*Frank*: No thank you, I don't wear them.

—*THE NAKED GUN*

"One's too many an' a hundred's not enough!"

—NAT THE BARTENDER, *THE LOST WEEKEND*

"You remember how it really was? You and me and booze: a threesome. You and I were a couple of drunks on the sea of booze, and the boat sank. I got hold of something that kept me from going under, and I'm not going to let go of it. Not for you. Not for anyone. If you want to grab on, grab on. But there's just room for you and me: no threesome."

—JOE CLAY, *DAYS OF WINE AND ROSES*

*Susan*: A *real* woman could stop you from drinking.
*Arthur*: It'd have to be a real *big* woman.

—*ARTHUR*

## THE DRINKS CABINET
In the 2006 remake of the James Bond thriller *Casino Royale*, Agent 007 orders a very particular kind of martini: "Three measures of Gordon's; one of vodka; half a measure of Kina Lillet. Shake it over ice, and add a thin slice of lemon peel." Bond later christens the drink a Vesper Martini, after his ill-fated romance with Vesper Lynd: "Because once you've tasted it," he tells Lynd, "that's all you want to drink." How charming. Bond orders and names this same drink in the original Ian Fleming novel

*Casino Royale*. Kina Lillet, in case you don't know, is a French aperitif made of Bordeaux wines and citrus liqueurs. Served chilled, Lillet is often drunk on ice with a twist of lemon, lime, or orange.

"Wanna know how I got these scars? My father was . . . a *drinker*."

—THE JOKER, *THE DARK KNIGHT*

## GET AWAY FROM ME, BOY, YA BOTHER ME!

Hollywood has never produced a souse so memorable, lovable, and iconic as W. C. Fields. In both film and radio, Fields was the embodiment of the drunk uncle, the wayward gambler, the good-for-nothing, the red-nosed gent who hated little kids, dogs, and women, especially those who hectored him for his habits. Fields gave the world countless hours of entertainment, as well as a wealth of memorable quotes.

"I always keep a supply of stimulant handy in case I see a snake—which I also keep handy."

—W. C. FIELDS

"Reminds me of my safari in Africa. Somebody forgot the corkscrew and for several days we had to live on nothing but food and water."

—W. C. FIELDS

"A woman drove me to drink and I never even had the courtesy to thank her."

—W. C. FIELDS

"A man's got to believe in something. I believe I'll have another drink."

—W. C. FIELDS

# "Somebody left the cork out of my lunch."

—W. C. FIELDS

"I never drink water. I'm afraid it will become habit-forming."

—W. C. FIELDS

"I never drink water; that is the stuff that rusts pipes."

—W. C. FIELDS

"The cost of living has gone up another dollar a quart."

—W. C. FIELDS

"You can't trust water: Even a straight stick turns crooked in it."

—W. C. FIELDS

## THE STARS ON DRINKING

W. C. Fields isn't the only actor who had something to say about drinking. Why do you think movie stars are called "the toast of the town"? It's because Hollywood runs on the hard stuff.

"Today, if you're not an alcoholic, you're nobody."

—DICK VAN DYKE

"I can't die until the government finds a safe place to bury my liver."

—PHIL HARRIS

"I made a commitment to completely cut out drinking and anything that might hamper me from getting my mind and body together. And the floodgates of goodness have opened upon me—spiritually and financially."

—DENZEL WASHINGTON

"The best audience is one that is intelligent, well-educated, and a little drunk."

—ALBEN W. BARKLEY

"When a woman drinks it's as if an animal were drinking, or a child. Alcoholism is scandalous in a woman, and a female alcoholic is rare, a serious matter. It's a slur on the divine in our nature."

—MARGUERITE DURAS

# "Do not allow children to mix drinks. It is unseemly and they use too much vermouth."

—STEVE ALLEN

"Alcohol doesn't console, it doesn't fill up anyone's psychological gaps, all it replaces is the lack of God. It doesn't comfort man. On the contrary, it encourages him in his folly, it transports him to the supreme regions where he is master of his own destiny."

—MARGUERITE DURAS

"When I played drunks I had to remain sober because I didn't know how to play them when I was drunk."

—SIR RICHARD BURTON

"I do not live in the world of sobriety."

—OLIVER REED

"Sobriety was the greatest gift I ever gave myself. I don't put it on a platform. I don't campaign about it. It's just something that works for me. It enabled me to really connect with another human being— my wife, Sheryl—which I was never able to do before."

—ROB LOWE

"A few years back I was more a candidate for skid row bum than an Emmy. If I hadn't stopped [drinking], I'd be playing handball with John Belushi right now."

—JOHN LARROQUETTE

"I always wake up at the crack of ice."

—JOE E. LEWIS

"I don't drink any more than the man next to me, and the man next to me is Dean Martin."

—JOE E. LEWIS

"I drink to forget I drink."

—JOE E. LEWIS

"It pays to get drunk with the best people."

—JOE E. LEWIS

*Dr. Hugo Pine*: I can drink any amount of alcohol I like and it doesn't bother me a bit.
*James Gannon*: Well it doesn't bither me a bot either!

—TEACHER'S PET

"God, I'd give anything for a drink. I'd give my goddamned soul for just a glass of beer."

—JACK TORRANCE, THE SHINING

"Christ, I'd do anything for a pint. I'd lick the sweat off a monkey's balls."

—FINN, TURISTAS

"Er, thank you, but you see, we Draculas don't drink wine."

—GRANDPA, THE MUNSTERS

"I woke up one morning, and when I looked in the mirror I noticed my nose was bent over entirely onto one side of my face. So, I got a hammer, and started banging my nose back to a right angle with my face. Suddenly, I looked at myself in the mirror, hammer in hand, blood streaming down my chin, and I realized my life was no longer manageable."

—RICHARD, CLEAN AND SOBER

*Michael Green*: My wife is an alcoholic. Best person I ever met. She has 600 different smiles. They can light up your life. They can make you laugh out loud, just like that. They can even make you cry, just like that. That's just with her smiles. You'd have to see her with her kids. You'd have to see how they look at her, when she's not looking. To think of all the things she lives through, and I couldn't help her.

*Alice Green*: Maybe helping wasn't your job.

—WHEN A MAN LOVES A WOMAN

*Ben Sanderson*: Don't you think you'd get a little bored, living with a drunk?

*Sera*: Well . . . that's what I want.

*Ben*: You haven't seen the worst of it. I knock things over . . . throw up all the time. These past few days I've been very controlled. You're like some sort of antidote that mixes with the liquor and keeps me in balance. But that won't last forever.

—LEAVING LAS VEGAS

"Do we need a two-and-a-half hour movie about the Doors? No, we don't. I can sum it up for you in five seconds, OK. I'm drunk. I'm nobody. I'm drunk. I'm famous. I'm drunk. I'm fucking dead. There's the whole movie, OK?"

—DENIS LEARY, *NO CURE FOR CANCER*

"I never drink . . . wine."

—DRACULA, *DRACULA*

"I never drink wine, and I do not smoke shit."

—DRACULA, *LOVE AT FIRST BITE*

"I never drink . . . wine. Oh, what the hell, let me try it."

—DRACULA, *DRACULA: DEAD AND LOVING IT*

*Lady Esme Hammond*: Sherry, Marya?

*Countess Marya Zaleska*: Thank you, I never drink . . . wine.

—DRACULA'S DAUGHTER

"I don't drink . . . coffee."

—DRACULA, *DRACULA 2000*

"You hear that, Herman, hm? The pride of Transylvania treated like a common criminal. Heh, Well, I'll tell ya, that's enough to drive a man to drink! Hm. Oh, what I wouldn't give for a nice Bloody Mary. Or Dorothy or Emily."

—GRANDPA MUNSTER,
THE MUNSTERS' REVENGE

"He's the first one to kill a vampire in over a hundred years. I'd say that's earned him a drink."

—ANNA VALERIOUS, VAN HELSING

## THE DRINKS CABINET

One of my favorite moments in the movie *The Blues Brothers* is when Jake and Elwood commandeer a table at a fancy restaurant and order the house's finest Champagne: when the sommelier approaches, Elwood holds out his water glass. "Wrong glass, *sir*," the sommelier says sternly, but Elwood will have none of it: Fill 'er up.

- One drinks Champagne out of a "**flute glass**" (tall and thin) or a "**coupe glass**" (short, shaped like a small bowl). Right out of the bottle is considered uncouth.
- A "**tumbler**" is a glass with a flat bottom, and in the field of mixed drinks, one has a "Collins glass" (10–14 fluid ounces), a "highball glass" (8–12 ounces), and an "Old Fashioned" glass (6–10 ounces). This latter glass is also known as a "lowball glass" or a "rocks glass," since drinks served in it tend to call for ice.
- A "**cocktail glass**" (4.5 ounces) is what martinis are served in, not in "martini glasses." And please, for the love of Anacreon, stay away from those cocktail glasses that are so big and wide, they look like they could contain half a dozen goldfish.

## CHAPTER 12

# OH, THE PLACES YOU'LL DRINK!

Sure, you save a lot of money by buying alcohol at the store and drinking it at home, but anyone can do that. By drinking out, you're paying for ambiance, local color, and good company. A beer drunk at home simply does not taste as good as one you order in a bar because your home team just took home the trophy. All homes are pretty much the same: living room, TV, kitchen, bathroom. Ah, but outside in the big wide world are dumps and dives, pubs and taverns, watering holes and licensed establishments: those are the places where history is made. No one ever made history in their living room. And without a bartender, who at home are you going to tell your troubles to? Your dog?

"Oh, you hate your job? Why didn't you say so? There's a support group for that. It's called *everybody*, and they meet at the bar."

—DREW CAREY, *THE DREW CAREY SHOW*

"A good bartender has to be part philosopher, part psychiatrist, part psychic."

—AL THE BARTENDER, *QUANTUM LEAP*

*Dave*: I like the sound the glass makes when the bartender puts it on the counter. I like the way it feels in my hand. I bring it in close, and I can smell it, and a wave of relief goes through my body even before I take the first sip.
*Billie*: You're slow. I'd be on my third one by now.

—*RUDE AWAKENING*

"Yeah, I know I'm ugly! I said to a bartender, 'Make me a zombie.' He said, 'God beat me to it.'"

—RODNEY DANGERFIELD

"Uh, listen Marge, um—how can I put this delicately? I don't got enough booze in this place to make you look good."

—BARTENDER MOE SZYSLAK, *THE SIMPSONS*

"I haven't seen you this upset since your bartender took early retirement."

—DR. SAMANTHA WATERS, *PROFILER*

## WATERING SPOTS

Most Americans see the inside of a bar well before legal drinking age, on account of the fact that the local tavern is a favored setting for TV sitcoms. Match the name of the fictional character to the name of his or her haunt.

1. Peter Griffin
2. Archie Bunker
3. Homer Simpson
4. Norm Peterson
5. Dr. "Hawkeye" Pierce
6. Jack Tripper
7. "Luke" and "Bo" Duke

- Moe's Tavern
- The Drunken Clam
- Rosie's Bar
- Kelsey's/Kelcy's Bar
- Boar's Nest
- Cheers
- The Regal Beagle

Answers: (1) Drunken Clam; (2) Kelsey's; (3) Moe's; (4) Cheers; (5) Rosie's; (6) Regal Beagle; (7) Boar's Nest.

"I went to the bartender, I said, 'Surprise me.' He showed me a naked picture of my wife!"

—RODNEY DANGERFIELD

*Frank [played by Zeppo Marx]:* Dad, two of the greatest football players in the country hang out in a speakeasy downtown!

*Prof. Wagstaff [Groucho Marx]:* Are you suggesting that I, the president of Huxley College, go into a speakeasy without even giving me the address?

—HORSE FEATHERS

"My parents' divorce settlement involved a bar tab."

—CHRISTOPHER TITUS, *NORMAN ROCKWELL IS BLEEDING* (TV MOVIE)

*Woody*: Pour you a beer, Mr. Peterson?

    *Norm*: All right, but stop me at one. Make that one-thirty.

—CHEERS

*Coach*: What's new, Norm?

    *Norm*: I need something to hold me over until my second beer.

    *Coach*: How about a first beer?

    *Norm*: That'll work.

—CHEERS

"I don't care how liberated this world becomes: a man will always be judged by the amount of alcohol he can consume. And a woman will be impressed, whether she likes it or not."

—BARTENDER DOUG COUGHLIN,<br />COCKTAIL

*Norm*: Morning, everybody!

    *Woody*: Beer, Mr. Peterson?

    *Norm*: Little early in the day isn't it, Woody?

    *Woody*: Little early for a beer?

    *Norm*: No, for stupid questions.

—CHEERS

*Fredo* [*having just arrived in Cuba*]: *Uno . . . por favor . . .* How do you say "banana daiquiri"?
*Michael*: "Banana daiquiri."

—THE GODFATHER: PART TWO

"Two things you need at a bar is ice and water: water for mixing drinks and ice to drop into people's shorts and into their hats, depending on where their hangover is."

—RED GREEN, THE RED GREEN SHOW

"This place has a sign hangin' over the urinal that says, "Don't eat the big white mint.""

—WADE GARRETT, ROAD HOUSE

## WATERING SPOTS

Drinkers of every stripe and taste dream of making a pilgrimage to where their favorite libation is made—the font from which their satisfaction springs! So get out your map, name your poison, and plan your next vacation:

- **The Jack Daniels Distillery** is 75 miles to the southeast of Nashville, TN, in Lynchburg.
- **Anheuser-Busch** has tourable breweries in five U.S. cities: St. Louis, MO; Jacksonville, FL; Fort Collins, CO; Fairfield, CA; and Merrimack, NH.
- **The Coors Brewery** is located (as you'd know from their commercials) in Golden, CO, which is 15 miles west of Denver.
- Boston may have its "Freedom Trail," but only Kentucky has the **Kentucky Bourbon Trail,** which ushers attendees to no fewer than six landmark distilleries: **Four Roses**; **Wild Turkey**; **Heaven Hill**; **Jim Beam**;

**Maker's Mark**; and **Woodford Reserve**.

- If you're going to Milwaukee, your first thought might be to tour a beer brewery: **Pabst**, **MillerCoors**, **Sprecher**, or the smaller **Milwaukee Brewing Company** and the **Lakefront Brewery**. But don't miss the tour at the **Great Lakes Distillery**, the city's first distillery since Prohibition. Ask how well their vodka, gin, absinthe, rum, or brandy go with bratwurst.
- Boston, MA, is always a nice family trip, and while the kids are at the Franklin Park Zoo or the verdant Arnold Arboretum, family members interested in a brew tour can head up the street a ways to the **Boston Beer Company**, where they brew **Sam Adams**.

"My wife and I have a tour bus on which we have three dogs, two of which are Scottish terriers, because if you drink enough Johnnie Walker products, eventually they just send you the dogs."

—RON WHITE, *BLUE COLLAR COMEDY TOUR: ONE FOR THE ROAD*

"He asks if you want a drink. You smile and say, 'Vodka soda.' If you already have a drink, you down it. Then there's some flirting, some interoffice sex, an accidental pregnancy, a shotgun wedding, and a life of bliss. How many times do we have to go over this?"

—CASEY, *27 DRESSES*

"Don't spill none of that liquor, son. It eats right into the bar."

—JUDGE ROY W. BEAN, *THE WESTERNER*

*Howard Wolowitz*: I'm not sitting here with a guy drinking a grasshopper with a little umbrella.

*Rajesh Koothrappali*: Fine. I'll have a chocolate martini.

*Howard*: Wrong again.

*Rajesh*: Come on, you know I can't talk to women unless I'm lit up like the Hindu festival of Diwali.

*Howard*: Look, there are plenty of bars in L.A. where you can order grasshoppers and chocolate martinis but you wouldn't have to because there are no women in them.

—*THE BIG BANG THEORY*

# "Hey, don't knock drunks in bars! It means they're not out driving."

—IKE GRAHAM,
*RUNAWAY BRIDE*

*Roger the Alien*: I need a drink. Where's the booze?

*Hayley*: There is no booze. Saudi Arabia is a dry country.

*Roger*: Seriously, where's the booze?

—AMERICAN DAD!

## WATERING SPOTS

One summer, my in-laws from Milwaukee got a time-share in my native state of Rhode Island, in the tony seaside town of Newport. My father-in-law said he heard that Newport's **White Horse Tavern** (26 Marlborough St.) was the oldest operating tavern in America: he suggested we "go over for a coupla beers." I couldn't blame my father-in-law for associating "oldest U.S. tavern" with suds and bratwurst, but I had to diplomatically explain that going to the White Horse would require three things he and I happened not to have on this vacation: a suit coat, a tie, and a giant wad of cash. Whereas a lot of "oldest running bars" in American cities are nineteenth century, the White Horse is seventeenth century: you'd practically expect your waiter to wear a powdered wig. Entrees average $40. Nice place? Absolutely. Romantic? You bet. Worth it? Yes. Wide-screen TV showing Packers game? Uh-uh. Dress to impress, and know what wine to order with duck or Beef Wellington.

*Major Strasser*: What is your nationality?
　*Rick*: I'm a drunkard.
　*Captain Renault*: That makes Rick a citizen of the world.

—CASABLANCA

"Hey look, mister. We serve hard drinks in here for men who want to get drunk fast, and we don't need any characters around to give the joint 'atmosphere.' Is that clear, or do I have to slip you my left for a convincer?"

—NICK, *IT'S A WONDERFUL LIFE*

# "I can't stay mad at you, Moe. You get me drunk!"

—HOMER SIMPSON TO HIS BAR-
TENDER, *THE SIMPSONS*

"People who really want to have a good time won't come to a slaughterhouse. And we've got entirely too many troublemakers here. Too many forty-year-old adolescents, felons, power drinkers, and trustees of modern chemistry."

—DALTON, *ROAD HOUSE*

**WATERING SPOTS**

A "milk bar" was a mid-twentieth-century grocery store or pharmacy where milk and milkshakes were served at a counter. British author Anthony Burgess corrupted this wholesome image in his novel *A Clockwork Orange* with the Kordova Milk Bar, the favored hangout of young Alex and his gang of "droogs" (friends). The word "kordova" means "cow" in Russian, and at this establishment, milk was laced with amphetamines and other drugs, priming its clientele for a night of "ultra-violence." In Stanley Kubrick's 1971 adaptation of *A Clockwork Orange*, "milk plus" is dispensed through a female mannequin's breast.

# INDEX

Marlowe, Philip (*Murder, My Sweet*), 162
Marlowe, Philip (*The Big Sleep*), 76
Marquis, Don, 94
*Married with Children*, 33, 34, 35
Martin, Dean, 173
Martin, Harvey, 171
Masefield, John Edward, 43
Masson, Thomas L., 179
Matthew (*NewsRadio*), 103
Maugham, W. Somerset, 214
Maupassant, Guy de, 55
*Maverick*, 59
Maxwell, Andrew (*Diary of the Dead*), 62
Mayo, Casey (*The Blue Gardenia*), 199
McCambridge, Mercedes, 137
McCarthy, Parnell (*Anatomy of a Murder*), 69
McCartney, Paul, 91
McCroskey, Steve (*Airplane!*), 106
McCullers, Carson, 63
McGarry, Leo (*The West Wing*), 140, 141, 148
McGillis, Kelly, 173
McGoorty, Danny, 169
McLaughlin, Mignon, 135
McLeod, Detective James (*Detective Story*), 200
Mead, 5
Meechum, Bull (*The Great Santini*), 128
*Memento*, 20
Mencken, H. L., 65, 180, 207, 219, 220
Menure, Agnes (*Relative Strangers*), 138
Mercer, Nick (*The Wedding Date*), 120
Merry and Pippin (*The Lord of the Rings: The Return of the King*), 34
Meviana, Rumi, 7, 167
Mickey (*After Alice*), 99
Mickey (*Family Guy*), 114
Middleton, Thomas, 43
Midler, Bette, 172
Mike (*High Society*), 157

Milk bars, 238
Miller, Henry, 117
Miller, J. P., 179
MillerCoors, 236
Milwaukee Brewing Company, 236
Mimosa, 72
Miner, Charles, 80
Molière, 23
Mollari, Londo (*Babylon 5*), 106
Monaco (France), 28
*The Money Pit*, 198
Montague, Lord (*The Unholy Night*), 82
Montgomery, Edward (*Dharma & Greg*), 119
Montgomery, George, 170
Montgomery Martinis, 209
Mork (*Mork and Mindy*), 62
Morris, Christopher (*Brass Eye*), 160
Morrison, Helen (*The Blue Dahlia*), 162
Morse, Chief Inspector (*Inspector Morse*), 202
*Moulin Rouge*, 160, 199
*Mrs. Doubtfire*, 147
Mull, Martin, 93
Mullaney, Rock (*Crossfire Trail*), 61, 196
*Munich*, 161
Munster, Grandpa [character], 226, 229
Mustum, 46
*My Little Chickadee*, 63, 99
*My Name is Earl*, 146, 150, 154, 192

Naboth, Jim (*The Squeeze*), 82
*The Naked Gun*, 222
Nanni, Gabriele, 177
Naples Winter Wine Festival, 189
Napoleon. *See* Bonaparte, Napoleon
Nash, Ogden, 120, 208
Nation, Carrie, 27
Nat the Bartender (*The Lost Weekend*), 193, 222
Newlove, Donald, 213
*NewsRadio*, 103, 198

Newton, Byron R., 79
Nick (*It's a Wonderful Life*), 238
Nietzsche, Friedrich, 20, 24, 215
Nigerian proverb, 12
Nikki (*Spread*), 130
Nina (*Just Shoot Me!*), 90
Norm (*Cheers*), 233
*Norman Rockwell is Bleeding*, 129–30, 133
Norse proverb, 25
Number One (*The Simpsons*), 123

O'Brien, Conan, 137
O'Brien, Flann, 95
O'Brien, Kate (*The Drew Carey Show*), 31
*The O.C.*, 128, 143, 182
*The Office*, 117, 122, 152, 192
O'Herlihan, Rex (*Rustler's Rhapsody*), 70
O'Malley, Austin, 178
O-Neh-Da Vineyards, 10
O'Neill, Eugene, 204, 211
Orangina, 72
O'Reilly, "Radar" (*M*A*S*H*), 61, 84
O'Rourke, Brian, 96
O'Rourke, P. J., 24, 67, 181, 208, 211
Orwell, George, 168
Osborne, Julian (*On the Beach*), 201
O'Sullivan, John Louis, 64
*The Other Guys*, 135
*The Other Sister*, 159
Otto the Bus Driver (*The Simpsons*), 145
Ovid, 45, 172
Owen, Richard, 72

Pabst Brewing Company, 236
*Paint Your Wagon*, 13, 129
Palahniuk, Chuck, 22, 207
*Pal Joey*, 181
Panaché, 28
"Pappy" Maverick (*Maverick*), 59
Paracelsus, 30
Parker, Dorothy, 52, 67

# DAILY BENDER

## Want Some More?

Hit up our humor blog, The Daily Bender, to get your fill of all things funny—be it subversive, odd, offbeat, or just plain mean. The Bender editors are there to get you through the day and on your way to happy hour. Whether we're linking to the latest video that made us laugh or calling out (or bullshit on) whatever's happening, we've got what you need for a good laugh.

If you like our book, you'll love our blog. (And if you hated it, "man up" and tell us why.) Visit The Daily Bender for a shot of humor that'll serve you until the bartender can.

Sign up for our newsletter at
## *www.adamsmedia.com/blog/humor*
and download our Top Ten Maxims No Man Should Live Without.